ROBERT BOLT

A MAN FOR ALL SEASONS

NOTES

COLES EDITORIAL BOARD

ABOUT COLES NOTES

COLES NOTES have been an indispensible aid to students on five continents since 1948.

COLES NOTES are available for a wide range of individual literary works. Clear, concise explanations and insights are provided along with interesting interpretations and evaluations.

Proper use of COLES NOTES will allow the student to pay greater attention to lectures and spend less time taking notes. This will result in a broader understanding of the work being studied and will free the student for increased participation in discussions.

COLES NOTES are an invaluable aid for review and exam preparation as well as an invitation to explore different interpretive paths.

COLES NOTES are written by experts in their fields. It should be noted that any literary judgement expressed herein is just that — the judgement of one school of thought. Interpretations that diverge from, or totally disagree with any criticism may be equally valid.

COLES NOTES are designed to supplement the text and are not intended as a substitute for reading the text itself. Use of the NOTES will serve not only to clarify the work being studied, but should enhance the reader's enjoyment of the topic.

ISBN 0-7740-3307-X

COLES PUBLISHING COMPANY
TORONTO—CANADA
PRINTED IN CANADA

Manufactured by Webcom Limited
Cover finish: Webcom's Exclusive **Duracoat**

CONTENTS

Bolt: Brief Biography

Robert Oxton Bolt was born in Manchester, on the 15th August 1924, the son of Ralph Bolt and his wife Leah. He was educated at Manchester Grammar School, which has given so many remarkable men to public life. But young Bolt as a schoolboy does not seem to have made the most of his early opportunities, and in 1941 he left school to become an office boy in the Sun Life Assurance Office, thereby recalling the first steps of two other English playwrights, John Drinkwater and R.C. Sherriff, who first made their careers in Insurance.

Bolt did not spend long in the insurance business, and in 1943 he matriculated at Manchester University; but soon the war overtook him and the three years until 1946 were spent in National Service in various places, including France. On his demobilisation he returned to Manchester University for three years, and he completed a post-graduate course at Exeter University in 1950.

On leaving the University he immediately took up school-teaching as a career, first at a village school in Bishopsteignton, Devon, and later as teacher of English Literature at Millfield School, Somerset, where he remained until 1958, when he gave up teaching for the uncertainties of free-lance writing.

He wrote several radio and television features and his experience with the BBC quickly established his claim to be one of the coming young men. His first play in the live theatre was *The Critic and the Hearth,* which was produced at the Oxford Playhouse. Almost immediately his script *Flowering Cherry* was accepted by a famous company in the West End, and was put on at the Haymarket Theatre, London, where it met with instant success. That this was no fluke was shown by a similar success in America at the Lyceum Theatre, New York.

Probably a good deal of the success was due to the first-class production and the acting of Sir Ralph Richardson, but Bolt again succeeded with his next play, *A Man for All Seasons*, which was produced in the West End, this time at the Globe Theatre, London. Once more in New York the work of the rising playwright met with an enthusiastic reception.

Robert Brustein, drama critic of *The New Republic*, Professor of English Literature at Columbia University and Dean of the School of Drama at Yale, explained the attraction of the play when he commented: "Compared with the historical plays of Anouilh and Osborne, it shows remarkable intelligence, historicity, theatrical ingenuity and good taste. I confess the work took me by surprise, for nothing in the *Flowering Cherry* prepared me for the kind of form and substance he handles with such authority here."

1960 was the year of production of *A Man for All Seasons*. In the same year another play from Bolt's portfolio was produced, *The Tiger and the Horse*, which had its première at the Queen's Theatre, London, thus justifying the writer's claim to the laureateship of the West End, the El Dorado of every young dramatist's dream.

Wisely resisting any temptation to "cash-in" on his new-found success, Bolt next turned his attention to film scripts, and his film *Lawrence of Arabia* won an important award in 1962. It may be said that Bolt was responsible also for the scenario and script of the adaptation to the screen of Boris Pasternak's *Dr. Zhivago*.

Neither of his next two plays won anything like the recognition of *A Man for all Seasons*. In *Gentle Jack*, Bolt produced a fantasy of a rather artificial nature, which reminded many spectators of Bernard Shaw's pantomime-play *Androcles and The Lion* and James Bridie's Barrie-like plays of whimsy-cum-argument, but it added little to Bolt's reputation.

He has been extremely fortunate in his interpreters; the country's leading stars—Ralph Richardson, Michael Redgrave, Edith Evans, Paul Scofield and others have appeared, ably supported by some of the foremost actors of the period; in this way he has been identified as a "Shaftesbury Avenue" dramatist, like Terence Rattigan and Noel Coward, rather than one of the playwrights who came to fame on the crest of John Osborne's sensationally successful *Look Back in Anger*.

Robert Bolt has been the Theatre's golden boy. It remains to be seen whether he will sustain that reputation. It may be mentioned that *A Man for All Seasons* gained an Oscar award for the best screen play of 1966. This film is a direct adaptation of the play, made by Bolt himself; awards to Paul Scofield for the best acting of the year, and to the film director Fred Zinnemann, were also made.

Robert Bolt is one of the new dramatists who have revolutionised the theatre in the mid-Twentieth Century. 8th May, 1956 is the most widely quoted date in recent theatrical history. For that day was the première of John Osborne's *Look Back in Anger*, which marked the beginning of a new era in British drama. The great days of the theatrical renaissance, the days of Shaw and Galsworthy, had given way to the rather artificial products of Frederick Lonsdale, Noel Coward, Terence Rattigan and a host of minor writers who largely catered to the fashionable "West End Theatre", that square mile of fashionable London bounded by Shaftesbury Avenue, Drury Lane and Covent Garden; there the fare was pretty much "the mixture as before". Occasionally it threw up a *bravura* writer like Christopher Fry, whose *Lady's not for Burning* is the all-time model for theatrical pyrotechnics, a mixture of whimsy, colour and verbal cadenzas. But generally the West End theatre played to a formula which James Bridie wittily defined as "two hours amidst the erotic misadventures of the English upper classes". This theatre was a class institution; it seemed it would last for ever. But in May 1956 its death knell was sounded. The vitality of Osborne spelled the end of this effete theatre—which had long been sickening from the dual effects of television and the cinema.

For years the greatest figures in English literature—men like James Joyce, Yeats and their equals had turned their backs on this type of theatre, with its vacuous audiences. Somerset Maugham had abandoned play-writing in despair.

Exactly what caused the sudden flurry, the excitement, the new life is uncertain. Possibly producers like George Devine and Joan Littlewood were responsible. Whatever the cause, good writers suddenly found that they were welcome in the new theatre. The theatre had become liberated. In quick succession playwrights like Arnold Wesker, Brendan Behan, Sheila Delaney, John Whiting, John Arden, Harold Pinter and Samuel Beckett emerged. The avant-garde of Continental writers made their appearance—Bertolt Brecht, Friedrich Dürrenmatt, Ionesco, Max Frisch, Albert Camus, Ugo Betti and others.

Fresh actors with new styles emerged. No longer was it essential to copy Gielgud and Olivier. The new stage had for its heroes actors like Paul Scofield, Leo McKern, Alan Bates, Alan Dobie, Richard Pascoe, Albert Finney, Peter O'Toole and producers like Peter Hall came to the fore. The mannered style of acting that saw its heyday in such performers as Rex Harrison, Ray Milland and Noel Coward gave way to the proletarian manliness of "Actors in the Raw". Well might the dowager in the stalls exclaim, "I never knew till now that Shakespeare's Romans spoke with a Liverpool accent".

It was all part of the theatrical shake-up, and suddenly all the old, stereotyped conventions and artificialities of the fashionable West End theatre gave way: Jimmy Porter's jazz trumpet blew away the old colonels and frowsy upper class hangers on. The genteel accents, the "posh" shibboleths faded overnight and all we seemed to hear in the theatre was the Cockney soldier in Behan's *Hostage* crying, "O Death Where is thy Sting-a-ling-a-ling"?

One thing was quite clear: amid all the confusion, the shouting and the revolutionary cries, the old type of theatre as an entertainment for genteel minds was definitely "out". The "Who's for Tennis" School had definitely taken a blow from which it never recovered. But the most important aspect of this revolution in taste was that it was genuine and real—it was not a palace revolution. For centuries the theatre had been the closely-guarded citadel, the preserve of the privileged few. It seemed that after 1956 the Bastille had fallen—and the stage was occupied by the works of dramatists like Sheila Delaney, whose educational background was Salford Hippodrome and the cinema three times a week; a girl of the under-privileged class, who, when invited to watch a performance of *Othello* at school, had confessed, "Anything for a laugh".

It was in his atmosphere that Robert Bolt first seized his chance. Yet he was not a typical "Angry young Man"; on the contrary he was very much an "Establishment" writer, a "find" of the last guard of the West End Theatre.

Life of Sir Thomas More

Thomas More was born in the city of London on February 6th, 1478, the second child in a *bourgeois* family, his father being John More, butler and steward at Lincoln's Inn, who later, in 1517, became a judge in the Court of King's Bench, and who died in 1530, only five years before his son's downfall.

Thomas went to St. Anthony's School, Threadneedle Street (1486), where he first learned the Latin for which he was renowned, and in which he was later to write one of the world's greatest documents—*Utopia* (1516). One must never forget that his own instruction was according to the pattern of the age of chivalry, and his education owes much to the fact that as a boy he was sent to the household of Cardinal Morton, at that time Lord Chancellor of England. There he learned the arts proper to a gentleman and early he was marked out: Cardinal Morton would often say to guests at table, "Mark that lad, one day he will prove a marvellous man". On the recommendation of Morton, More was later in 1492 sent to Canterbury Hall, Oxford (later absorbed in Christ Church College). We do not know precisely who his tutors were, although it is generally supposed that he learned Greek under Grocyn, and from Linacre. Certainly the climate of culture was that of the New Learning, and More's father was afraid that his son was going to be influenced by the new ideas, to the extent that he might abandon law, which had been chosen as his career. Therefore Thomas was recalled to London, according to Erasmus, where his father could supervise his studies. He was entered at an Inn of Chancery, and soon made his mark in law. He prospered so well that almost as soon as he was called to the bar he was appointed reader (i.e. lecturer or tutor) in law to the Faculty of Furnivall's Inn. He did not neglect his literary, philosophical and theological studies, however, for while still in his early twenties he delivered a series of lectures on St. Augustine in Dr. Grocyn's church of St. Laurence, Old Jewry. It was during this period that he became a friend of the world-famous scholar, Erasmus. In 1499 Erasmus paid his first visit to England and by the end of the year their friendship was firmly cemented.

As a young man, More had desired to enter the Church. For years he considered becoming a monk; and, indeed, until the last he used to mortify his flesh and wear a hair shirt. (This shirt was said to be one of the relics treasured by the Augustines of Abbot's Leigh in Somerset). Finally he decided against a monastic vocation: to use the words of Erasmus, he preferred to be a chaste husband rather than an impure monk. (The period of this dedication to a monkish life was 1499 to 1503.)

In 1504 he was elected to Parliament, and the following year he married; his first marriage was short-lived, lasting only four years, and after his wife's death he remarried—and it is this second wife, Alice, who figures in the play by Robert Bolt. 1509, the year of Henry VIII's accession to the throne, was the beginning of More's rise to eminence.

At first he acquired fame as a pleader or advocate in the courts; he was soon earning substantial sums, and his income has been estimated at the equivalent of £10,000 of today's money. In short, he was clearly established as one of the leaders of the Bar. He was soon elected Bencher of Lincoln's Inn, and in 1510 became the Under-Sheriff of the City of London. He was engaged as one of the counsel in a famous suit against the Crown and attracted the attention of the young King, and very soon he was pressed into the King's service, at first as Ambassador to Flanders, where he soon satisfied Wolsey that he possessed an alert brain and considerable ability for undertaking matters of state. In 1516 he wrote *Utopia*; and in the same year his friendship with Henry VIII began to ripen. Henry was at this time not the gross despot of later years but a handsome young prince who took all knowledge for his province, a fluent linguist, an expert on the lute and harpsichord, a capable athlete—in short a promising philosopher-king; truly a monarch who passionately identified himself with the New Learning and all that it implied.

In the light of what we now know, we are inclined to look on More's early relationship with Henry as something of an intellectual trap. With the hindsight of history, we think of More as the intellectual companion of Erasmus. In fact he was the everyday friend of the up-and-coming prince; they enjoyed each other's company and spent hours in argument and discussion. Not that More was deceived by the friendship of great princes. "The king walks arm in arm with me. But I have no cause to be proud. For if my head would win him a castle in France, it should not fail to go." Clearly, More was under no illusions, as this remark to Roper, his son-in-law, shows.

The King was a frequent guest in More's home at Chelsea, where More had bought a mansion in 1523. He often dined there, without notice, and shared something of the family life of More. It is interesting to recall that in this very family circle, where the King was a frequent "friend of the family", the youngest daughter Cecily later married a man who was to become foreman of the jury which sent Anne Boleyn to the block—as one of More's biographers remarks, surely a coincidence that no historical novelist would dream of contriving!

In 1529, Wolsey, the most hated man in England, fell from power and the land rejoiced. Thomas More had served under him, and had a thorough knowledge of the circumstances which had laid Wolsey low. More was created Lord Chancellor in his place—the first layman in England ever to become Lord Chancellor— "Keeper of The Conscience of the King." With this appointment the vested interest in the King's affairs by the church was arrested. The choice was popular—More was known as a ceaseless critic of corruption; as a judge he had never been known to take a bribe. He was the natural man to call on. He justified the choice, and for the first time the business of the courts was despatched with regularity and utter fairness. Soon after More had taken up office, the King's pressure began to be exercised. He dearly wanted the divorce that Wolsey had failed to negotiate. The Lord Chancellor asked the King to forgive him. From that moment More was at variance with the King's policy and in turn he was doomed. Realising that More would not yield, the King was forced to choose other advisers, and his eye turned on Thomas Cromwell, a crafty and calculating disciple of Machiavelli who bore no love for More. It is not necessary for our purpose to trace the steps which led to More's forfeiting the Great Seal. It is sufficient to note that in 1532 he left office a poor man—a fact which speaks eloquently of his incorruptibility. He was voted a sum of £5,000 in recognition of his work—which he declined. Yet if he thought to avoid a cruel fate, he was mistaken. Henry held the view that "He that is not with me is against me". More's absence from the Coronation of Anne Boleyn as Queen was carefully noted both by Cromwell and his royal master. From that moment the contest became a matter of personal rancour and intrigue.

The first signs were manifest in an attempt to charge More with accepting bribes. But the circumstances were so well-known, and More was so obviously incorruptible, that this charge was refuted almost as soon as it was made.

Again More realised that his enemy would never be satisfied till his head rolled in the dust. "What is postponed is not finished", he told his daughter Margaret. In March 1534 a bill made the authority of the Pope in England invalid, and everyone was called upon to swear an oath of Supremacy—to the effect that Henry and not the Pope or his Deputy was Head of the Church. It was this that More refused to acknowledge. As a lawyer, he took refuge in every legal defence that he could—but he would not swear to a spurious oath. Persisting in his refusal, he was committed to the Tower on 17th April, 1534. The proceedings dragged on until July 1535, where he was tried before a packed jury at Westminster Hall. Even then the Crown had to rely on the evidence of perjured testimony—the perjurer being Rich, the very man who in his younger days had been helped by More. As a result of this perjury, More was found guilty of treason and he was duly executed on 7th July, 1535. His judicial murder did not satisfy the Defender of the Faith, Henry VIII. The small property that More left was confiscated, and his widow was driven from it. Every penny was settled on the Princess Elizabeth, daughter of Anne Boleyn, who grimly held on to every penny to her dying day.

Perfection, it has been said, is not given to Man; and More would never have claimed to be perfect. But, a frail and ascetic, kindly soul, he was one of the very few who would not swear to what he did not believe. He went to his death for his conscience. The shock which his execution caused throughout the Christian world was the measure of his incomparable status.

On the 29th January, 1935 the Pope declared More to have been a martyr, and beatified, and in May of that year he formally canonised Thomas More as Saint. By a curious irony, the day, 19th May, was the anniversary of Anne Boleyn's death.

In studying a historical play, It is arguable how far the reader or spectator is helped to understand the plot or background by a study of the historical facts. Certainly the dramatic formula is rather like a "lightning sketch". The dramatist relies on a pre-knowledge of the theme and period, rather as an audience of ancient Greeks could be relied on to know the myths on which Euripides, Aeschylus and Sophocles worked. But the fact remains that the play will not yield up its secrets to those who are content to read it casually. Much background information is necessary to supplement the details merely indicated in the text of the play.

Therefore some acquaintance with the primary sources of the history of the period, and More's life in particular will be valuable—if only for reference. It is only recently that a transcript of the trial of More has been available, edited by E.E. Reynolds. More took his defence from the text of the statutes under which he was indicted, in his belief (misguided as it happened) that the letter of the law would be observed, even though the spirit was not. More believed in the Integrity of the Law, the Liberty of the individual under that law. That he was defeated is not attributable to his failure to appreciate the law so much as his failure to allow for perjury.

The main sources of More's biography rest on the *Lives* by William Roper, son-in-law and an important character in the play, and also that by Nicholas Harpsfield. The letters of Erasmus are invaluable for an appreciation of More's character, although in fact they refer to the earlier period in More's life. Roper's *Lives* was not published until 1626; nearly a century had to elapse before it was considered safe to write about the events that earlier shook a dynasty. Details about the political background can be found in Brewer's *Reign of Henry VIII.*

But the leading biography of More was Father T.E. Bridgetts' *Life of the Blessed Thomas More,* and a somewhat garbled life by More's descendant Cresacre More. Nicholas *Harpsfield's Life* edited by E.V. Hitchcock and R.W. Chambers, the standard work for scholars, was last published in 1932. The State papers of the period, edited by J.S. Brewer and J. Gairdner are available; and other material bearing on the Papal question is at hand in A.F. Pollard's *Henry VIII.* Earlier authorities, such as Sir James Mackintosh's *Life* (1844), will normally be consulted only by students of the period anxious to master the minute details.

Advanced students might like to take a glance at the play *The Tragedy of Sir Thomas More* which was edited by A. Dyce for the Shakespeare Society.

More recent books on More are Leslie Paul's *More* (Faber, 1953) and Richard L. Smith, *More* (Sheed and Ward, 1935). Jean Plaidy has written a historical novel, *St. Thomas's Eve,* on the period.

Story

Bolt says that he tried for a story rather than a plot. The play is loosely thrown into the form of what used to be called The Chronicle play, of which perhaps the greatest leading example in recent years has been John Drinkwater's *Abraham Lincoln*. From time to time the theatre throws up a recrudescence of this episodic form, with results mostly indifferent. Plays like Anouilh's *L'Alouette* (Joan of Arc) and T.S. Eliot's *Murder in the Cathedral* (Becket), Albert Camus's *Caligula,* Norman Ginsburg's *First Gentleman* (George IV), Bernard Shaw's *Saint Joan* are all examples of a *genre* that has from time to time, however, given us outstanding works.

As it happened, in the 1960's there was quite a spate of historical dramas in the London theatre: Terence Rattigan's *Ross* (Lawrence of Arabia) and John Osborne's *Luther* have shown that there was always an audience for the new interpretation of historical figures; and one of the "best sellers" of the theatre in between the wars had been Gordon Daviot's *Richard of Bordeaux*, a romantic conception of a historical figure.

What has to be remembered is that a historical play is not to be regarded as a theatrical presentation of history. In other words the dramatist does not set up in rivalry with the historian. His purpose is not historical but a psychological interpretation.

Nor must objective accuracy in the presentation of events be expected. The overriding consideration must always be the dramatic conception. The dramatist is not concerned with the niceties of historical fact but rather with the broad sweep of events. To this end he may ignore the calendar; he may find it necessary to transpose events, to telescope them, to alter dates so as to bring them within some sort of dramatic unity.

In *A Man for All Seasons* Robert Bolt has allowed himself the licence that is the latitude of the creator. He is not concerned with mere accuracy: he is not an archaeologist of Tudor events, and the student must not go to the play expecting to see a dramatic transcription of the latest historical research.

The best known historical play is probably *Henry V* by Shakespeare, and it will be a useful scholastic exercise to compare the structure of *Henry V* with Bolt's play. In both plays a number of short episodes are linked together; these episodes are in the main founded on historical fact, but in order to secure variety some latitude is allowed so that the play illustrates varied aspects of the "hero". It is obvious that no play could present the full biographical facts, so that the dramatist is forced to select and simplify—and to that extent every historical play must be a distortion of precise history. He selects according to his purpose or theme.

Nevertheless the principles of construction are broadly the same. In the place of Shakespeare's Chorus, Bolt presses into service The Common Man, about whom we shall have more to say presently. On the occasion of the original first performance in London, on 1st July 1960, the programme carried a note by the playwright.

> The action of this play ends in 1535, but the play was written in 1960; and if in production one date must obscure the other it is 1960 which I would clearly indicate to occupy the stage. The *life* of a man like More offers a number of caps which, in this or any other century, we may try on for size.

From that remark we can gather a clue as to what kind of play *A Man for All Seasons* is. It is a play, using St. Thomas More as titular symbol, which is concerned with a theme that is eternal: how far along the road of what is called expediency (Shakespeare in *King John* called it commodity) a man may go before he is brought to a halt; to the point where something that we can call conscience steps in and says, "Thus far, and no further". More did not want to be a martyr; for a time he relied on all the quibbles of legality, he took refuge in every trick in the lawyer's book; but in the last analysis he saw his position quite clearly. The play is really a study of passive resistance against authoritarianism. It is a dilemma that is always with us—sometimes in the form of high comedy, sometimes of profound tragedy.

As in Shaw's *Saint Joan*, the dramatist has been scrupulously fair; apart from Henry VIII, there are no real villains in this piece. As Shaw said, "A villain in a play can be nothing better than a *diabolus ex machina*...possibly a more exciting expedient than a *deus ex machina*, but both equally mechanical, and therefore interesting only as a mechanism".

The play begins at the moment when More is to all intent firmly entrenched as Master of Requests, a form of judgeship; he was not yet Lord Chancellor, and Wolsey was still in the ascendant. But already two men appear who will play a great part in the later scenes of the drama: Richard Rich, who is so unimportant that More's Steward can afford to dismiss him as a mere nonentity; later he is to be the Solicitor-General who perjures himself to secure More's conviction; the other man is Thomas Cromwell—who is mentioned at first only as a student of Machiavelli.

As has been indicated, the play is enacted through a series of episodes, played continuously, and between them the changes of scene are bridged by the device of the appearance of The Common Man who plays a number of small parts of minor importance which link together these successive episodes. The importance of this stage character will be discussed in detail later. Suffice it here to say that he is something of a "Brechtian" Chorus—who plays all the lower-class characters, a greedy opportunist who takes every chance to point out that "It isn't difficult to keep alive—just don't make any trouble". This character is clearly modelled on the Story Teller in Bertolt Brecht's *Caucasian Chalk Circle*, and perhaps he owes something as well to the ever-present Narrator in sound radio plays, bearing in mind that Bolt served an apprenticeship as BBC script-writer and dramatic producer.

The relevance of the play lies in the fact that, though times change, men remain the same; psychological motives remain constant. There are despots now, as there were in 1535; there were men who were prepared to swear to anything then as now.

The printed play is divided into two acts. But for the purposes of studying the play, it will be convenient to split the text of each act into a number of smaller scenes or episodes, bearing in mind that the action runs continuously without pause, save for the incursion, at intervals, of the Common Man who steps on to the stage, partly to stage-manage the properties, and partly to comment on the action—a combination of epic and dramatic methods. When Garrick produced Shakespeare's *Henry V*, he chose to play the role of Prologue—and it may be that many spectators will think the Common Man is an equally attractive acting role.

The play is not concerned with More's earlier life. For example, no one would ever suspect that More was one of the leaders of the humanist movement in England; or that he was a satirist whose *Utopia* is one of the world's important literary documents; or that he was the scourge of heretics. The play is almost exclusively concerned with More as a symbol of passive resistance.

Theme

William Archer, one of the greatest English dramatic critics, once said that the first step towards writing a play was to choose a theme. But he admitted that such a simple statement required careful examination before its full import was grasped.

The theme of Bolt's play may conveniently be said to be passive resistance. The dramatist himself has written, "It is not easy to know what a play is about until it is finished, and by then what it is 'about' is incorporated in it irreversibly and is no more to be separated from the work as a whole than the shape of a statue is to be separated from the marble".

The theme of many great plays may be stated—quite frequently in a single word: thus the theme of *Othello* is jealousy; that of *Tartuffe* is hypocrisy; the theme of *Getting Married* is matrimony. In this narrow sense almost every play may be said to have an ethical overtone, more or less explicit, which may be stated sometimes in the case of a proverb, such as Ostrovsky's *Poverty is no Crime*; indeed, many plays are no more than a dramatic statement of a proverb. Yet in others it is impossible to state the theme in terms of a single abstraction. While it is quite possible to lay one's finger on the essence of the play and declare that to be the theme, this has little practical effect on the play's interpretation.

This play most certainly did not arise through a conscious process of selection, followed by the choice of the More story as an illustration. The dramatist did not say, "I will arise now and write a play about passive resistance—a play of protest about the necessity of not submitting to the establishment—and I will take Henry VIII and Anne Boleyn as an illustration".

Indeed Bolt is not a dramatist of protest in the ordinary acceptance of the phrase at all. It is true that, as Harold Hobson comments in the Penguin edition of this play. "Men and women are much more political animals nowadays than Aristotle supposed them to be". Detachment from the political scene is no longer possible since modern weapons overshadow life everywhere. "The problem facing Neville Harrison, Thomas More and Urbain Grandier [the heroes of three plays considered by Harold Hobson] is essentially the same problem. They are at grips with forces immeasurably greater than themselves. They exist in the twentieth century and in the sixteenth century—the impossibility of leading private lives." The ivory tower is no longer a permissible retreat.

This is the view of the theme that first attracted the dramatist. More was a famous man; not under-privileged, but a man who would generally be thought of as belonging to the privileged classes. Even so, he saw that without a certain something life was valueless. That certain something was a belief in "a power above ourselves"—a belief in the scruples of conscience. He knew that one cannot whittle away conscience. Far from being a martyr, he was timid. But in the last resort, he could face up to the most monstrous tyranny rather than submit to blasphemy. And the swearing of an oath knowing it to be blasphemy was exactly that:

> More was a very orthodox Catholic and for him an oath was something perfectly specific. It was an invitation to God,...the consequence of perjury was damnation....So for More the issue was simple (though remembering the outcome it can hardly have been easy). (Preface.)

The essential conflict of the play lies between the powers that represent giving way to blasphemy, and More's personal integrity—his belief in the inviolability of the Oath. It is symbolical of the conflict that seems doomed everlastingly to take place whenever vested authority is challenged by the pure in heart.

Yet the play is not a dramatic illustration of a mere text-book moral. The plays of Galsworthy such as *Strife* and *Justice* represent a Hegelian struggle of thesis and antithesis. They are purely logical working out of theoretical or abstract propositions. They are sociological plays. But *A Man for All Seasons* is not cut and dried dramatisation of a Parliamentary report.

The starting point of the play is found in the character of Thomas More. Indeed, without that character, the theme itself would be arid and dry. Independent of character, passive resistance would be a very uninteresting conflict indeed.

To many readers of the play and spectators in the audience, it may seem strange that More was so stubborn about what may seem a mere interpretation of religious dogma. The play may seem to be a revival of "battles long ago", but to take this view would be to minimise the importance of the theme. More was concerned with human liberty.

Once Carlyle spoke rather contemptuously about the Athanasian controversy, and likened it to the Christian world torn to pieces over a diphthong: but later he acknowledged that in this controversy—evidently about a diphthong—the entire meaning of Christianity was at stake. If the Arians had won, Christianity would have been lost.

So it may be that on a very technical point the entire reality of a doctrine may exist. In one sense it may seem to us, centuries afterwards, that the conflict between Henry VIII and the Church of Rome was an academic exercise, and may not have seemed worth the sacrifice of a single life. But deeper reflection will show that the struggle was a classic pattern of the struggle between forces of crucial importance. More defended the paramount authority of the collective Church against individual judgment. This controversy in fact had decisive effects on the national heritage.

What many present day students cannot understand is the respect that More had for Henry VIII as King. To understand this properly, we must rid ourselves of the popular image of Henry.

More was a pre-Reformation Roman Catholic. That is, he believed mankind should be subject to hierarchy. The very word is suspect nowadays: but to More Christian life was unthinkable without a system of hierarchy—the divine law of subordination and mutual dependence of the different ranks of created beings, human and angelical.

To most of us, brought up on democratic notions, the philosophy of hierarchies is quite unacceptable. William Morris's aphorism, "No man is good enough to be another man's master", is now the prevailing philosophical theory—even if it is not the practice. The doctrine of hierarchy—the Great Chain of Being—seems too much like the Victorian attitude of:

> The rich man in his castle,
> The poor man at his gate,
> God made them high and lowly
> And ordered their estate.

The order in heaven was reproduced on earth, and the king corresponded with the sun. This was Platonic doctrine, and failure to comply with the system, failure to acknowledge it, to give to Caesar that which was Caesar's, would undoubtedly result in chaos. So to be a true subject of the King was a proper duty of a Catholic citizen. Despite the efforts of latter day critics to identify More with the theories he preached satirically in *Utopia*, he was in no sense a political revolutionary. His whole attitude was one of compliance with universal law.

As a Historical Play

Because the theme of the play is set in remote historical times, the play is loosely described as "historical". Bolt says that "I took a historical setting in the hope that the distance of years would give me Dutch courage, and enable me to treat my characters in a properly heroic, properly theatrical manner".

When we speak of a historical play do we refer to the political background of the times in which the play is set and to which it refers? Or is the historical background just chosen by the playwright because it is vivid and colourful, affording opportunity for spectacle and costume? Do the audience who witness a historical play go to the theatre in the hope of seeing a serious examination of the politics of the period? Or do they interpret the play as a kind of allegory on present times, set amid the framework of a historical past? The question is one on which the student will have to make up his own mind: it is impossible to generalise usefully. Historical plays vary enormously, in subject-matter, treatment, depth—some are realistic, some are romantic; some are loaded beneath a weighty cargo of archaeological research—others are patently fiction to which a thin veneer of historical authenticity has been added. Indeed, history itself is a subject which has undergone steady revaluation; the difference in attitude between the historian of the school of Namier, Toynbee and Butterfield, is quite different from that of, say, Macaulay and J.R. Green.

The one common denominator of all the plays that could be collected together under the label "historical" is that they should be actable and that they should "popularise" history, that is to say they should have a distinct entertainment value, at different levels of intelligence. The aim of the playwright is to present historical episodes with an imaginative vision. The most obvious fact is that history offers colourful and stirring scenes on which the dramatist can fasten his attention. Put briefly, the attraction of the history play is that it presents ready-made the ingredients of tragedy, comedy and melodrama. On the other hand its limitations are that the writer is bound by information already at hand. Distortion of historical characters there may be, but in the main the writer is confined to the popular "image" of the historical character whom he seeks to portray. The theatre, as William Archer once remarked, is not the place to present original research, or to present new interpretations of character.

For example, everyone knows that the popular image of Richard III as a Machiavellian villain is largely a myth, credited partly to Shakespeare, partly to More as historian, and partly to the Tudor need for blackening the usurper's character. As long ago as Horace Walpole, formidable doubts concerning this popular view of Richard had been recorded: for instance, the view that he was a loathsome hunchback has given way to the more accurate view that his physique was the off-shoot of an attack of what would now be called polio-myelitis. But for theatrical purposes Richard has been painted a villain, and a villain he remains.

> The theatre is not the place for whitewashing Richard. It is not the place for proving that Guy Fawkes was an earnest Presbyterian or that Nell Gwynne was a strict moralist...the playwright who presents Henry VIII is bound to present him, as the schoolboy said, as a great widower. William the Silent must not be a chatter-box, nor Torquemada a humanitarian...where historic legend exists, he must respect it at his peril. (William Archer)

Legendary and historcal characters necessarily remain very much the creatures of myth that they have always been. A Napoleon who was not a military genius would be useless for dramatic purposes. Lloyd Osbourne's play *The Exile* failed in the theatre because it presented a view of Napoleon that no one could accept—a Napoleon in decline. It is quite likely that Napoleon, in later years, *was* in decline. But a theatrical audience is in no mood for such an uncharacteristic view. It wants to see the Napoleon of tradition. The scholar who is saturated in the history of the French revolution may know that the current image of Robespierre as a dreadful tyrant is wholly mistaken; but no dramatist has been found to take that view.

The aim of historical drama is not to probe truth, cost what it may in terms of popular acceptance. "Not truth, but verisimilitude is the dramatist's aim." When Bernard Shaw, defending his historical play *Good King Charles*, claimed that in *Saint Joan* and *Caesar and Cleopatra* he had been so accurate in his documentation that examination students could take these plays and be sure of passing, he was jesting.

It follows then that we must not expect a revaluation of the character of More. Perhaps the only example of a drama constructed on a revolutionary reinterpretation of a historical character is Strindberg's *Erik the Fourteenth*, the play about the epileptic monarch who unsuccessfully proposed to Queen Elizabeth I of England. Strindberg took a minority view of Erik's character—but the play has never found success in Sweden, although it was favourably received in Moscow, where its radical sentiments coincided with the atmosphere of the Soviets.

Surprisingly Robert Brustein finds "a faithful account of More's martyrdom, yet too diffuse to be entirely successful, yet compared with more vulgarly dramatic biographies like Anouilh's *Becket* and John Osborne's *Luther* it shows remarkable accuracy and good taste."

Brustein has summarised the play thus: "More, whose conversation according to Erasmus was full of jesting and fun, has usually been treated on the stage as a madcap: the Elizabethan play *Sir Thomas More*—erroneously ascribed at one time to Shakespeare—even has him cracking jokes on the scaffold. Bolt interprets him more as a melancholy intellectual aristocrat desperately trying to preserve some corner of private conscience, while preserving his life at the same time. More is prudent and discreet ('our natural business lies in escaping') and inclined to protect himself behind legalistic subterfuges. When asked to swear to the Acts of Succession, establishing Henry's divorce and his control over the English Church, he simply maintains silence. Determined not to be a martyr if he can help it, he could probably defend his strategy with the same aphorism as Brecht's Galileo - 'Unhappy is the land that needs a hero'. He is nudged into heroism reluctantly when all the escape routes have been closed. More's death, the wages of integrity, is for all ages...but the moral is for our time."

Voltaire said that "the history of the great movements of this world is nothing more than the history of crimes"; and when we remember the roll of martyrs in Tudor times we are inclined to agree; the role of the historical playwright is to provide a contemporary scale of reference for ages past. In the true sense of the word history is, as Bolingbroke said, philosophy teaching by examples. This play is essentially a facet of biography ; Bolt would agree with Emerson that there is no history without biography. History was the favourite reading of men like Napoleon, Lloyd George, Churchill and Hitler. And dramatised history was the favourite spectacle of the Elizabethans, who held with Bacon that "The purpose of history is to make men wise".

The crux of the play concerns the Oath of Supremacy and it is essential to follow the action closely, and to understand precisely the reasons why More was unable to subscribe to the Oath.

Early in 1533 Anne Boleyn was secretly married to Henry VIII. Cranmer, who had succeeded Warham as Archbishop of Canterbury, pronounced the King's marriage with Catherine of Aragon null and void, and the new Queen was crowned in June. More was conspicuous by his absence. His absence provoked the undying anger of both Anne and

Henry.

In 1534, the succession to the Crown was vested in the heirs of this marriage. In the preamble to the Act of Succession, the King's marriage with Catherine was expressly stated to be null and void, and his marriage with Anne was stated to be valid. All the King's subjects were required to swear this Oath—and Cromwell and Norfolk were appointed Commissioners to ensure that the swearing was carried out. Parliament took the oath on 30th March, 1532. This oath was regarded as the test of loyalty to Henry, and any who did not take it thus drew attention to their disloyalty—and hence, their treason. More then knew himself to be in the gravest danger. Attempts to implicate him in accepting bribes, and in being concerned in the affair of the "Holy Maid of Kent" (who had prophesied that anyone who supported the divorce was no longer a Catholic) failed; but the Oath could not be overcome by any legal means. More was now in peril of his life. On 12th April he was required to appear before the commissioners at Lambeth for the purpose of swearing the Oath. He refused. All attempts to persuade More to alter his mind failed. On 1st July he was formally brought to trial. On 7th July he was executed. When news of his death was brought to the King, he cast his eye on Anne Boleyn and said, "You are the cause of this"—and leaving the table, fell into a fit of melancholy.

So died the man whom Dean Swift described as a "man of the greatest virtue this kingdom has ever produced".

Style

So far as style is concerned, the play is not particularly noteworthy. There is no great regard for words, or any unusual technique in their handling. Unlike Harold Pinter, Bolt does not show any specific interest in using words as a theatrical vehicle. The vocabulary is adequate, but not in itself strikingly impressive. There are no speeches that the student feels impelled to learn by rote for the sake of their beauty. Even in the speeches of More there is nothing that is specifically striking. When the role was first played by Paul Scofield in London, it was noteworthy because he rarely raised his voice, and only in the final trial scene did he rely on vocal effect. Obviously the play is written with a view to ensemble playing. This is another point of technique that Bolt probably learned from Brecht. Solo performance, *prima donna* acting is frowned upon; the team-effect is what matters.

The visual appearance and a thumb-nail sketch of each character is given in Bolt's notes on "People in the Play". Here Bolt does not copy the technique of Bernard Shaw and Barrie and incorporate his characters' appearance in the stage directions, but the effect is the same. By giving an authoritative character before we have seen the characters in action or heard their words the dramatist dictates our views. Half the joy of seeing (or reading) a play is to speculate on the characters and to see what life means to them from their words, actions and influence in the play. The dramatist who provides us with his official version of their characters takes away that pleasure and , incidentally, makes his work less dramatic. It is obviously unnecessary (except for a producer) to give a description of the dress and appearance of a character who appears on the stage for all to see.

There is nothing specifically individual or characteristic that can be taken as marking Bolt's "finger prints". In a play of Wilde or Coward or Maugham, the lines sparkle and scintillate so that the authorship is instantly obvious. Often indeed in the works of these playwrights epigrams tend to come independently of the character supposed to be speaking them. The characters are in fact but the mouthpiece of the author. The spectators throng the playhouse to hear these lines spoken. But there is nothing remotely like that in *A Man for All Seasons*. Indeed, there is scarcely a memorable theatrical line from beginning to end. Like that of Drinkwater's *Abraham Lincoln*, the dialogue is threaded with homespun conversation, and the attraction of the play lies in its subject-matter, not in the form of its presentation. There are no long set speeches, no soliloquies, no verbal rhapsodies such as the twenty-minute oration in Cocteau's *The Eagle has Two Heads*, or the long involved arguments of the Inquisitor in *Saint Joan* of Shaw. The scenes fade into one another rapidly and are held together only by the Common Man who appears, as it were, to bridge the gap. Indeed his function often appears deliberately to lower the temperature rather than to raise it.

Shaw's characters are often "larger than life"—they are wittier than the people they represent would be. Not so with Bolt; never does he set out to move the audience with words. More often do his words move in pointed twos and threes.

Bolt has always the stage picture clearly before him. Every theatrical effect has been cleverly thought out, and the stage effects are always part of the creation and play a large part in the play's success (*e.g.* the lighting effects throughout).

Historical faithfulness is not the main concern in this play. Faithfulness to the past, in the sense of naturalism and regard for authenticity, is not of the first importance. It might be thought that faithfulness to the past would be the primary consideration of every historical dramatist, but this is not so.

Perhaps it will be helpful to quote in this connection a comment of Goethe, himself a foremost practitioner of the art of historical plays, such as *Egmont* and *Goetz von Berlichingen*. Goethe is dealing with the question of dialogue in Manzoni's historical tragedy, *Aldechi*:

> I pronounce in Manzoni's defence what may seem to be a paradox. Whenever we evoke in the past, in order to recite it after our own fashion to a contemporary audience, we translate the antique event. To all ancient conditions one lends a modern spirit, for only through modern ears can we hear and understand old things.

It was Hegel who said that anachronism was necessary to historical art: "The inner substance of what has to be represented remains the same, the change being that the modern culture necessitates a change in expression."

In other words a modern audience must have a historical theme served in the atmosphere and outlook of modern times. Mere deference to historical accuracy is not enough. For example, it does not help the audience one iota if the actual historical background is presented in all its archaeological *minutiae*. The material has to be recast so that attitudes and ideas become clear to people trained in a later way of expression and understanding.

Thus Scott, writing of the problems of a historical novelist (the problems of the novelist and playwright are almost identical): "It is true that I neither can pretend nor do to the observation of complete accuracy, even in important points of language. But the same motive which prevents my writing in Norman French or Anglo Saxon, or which prevents my using the typography of Caxton or Wynken de Worde, prevents my attempting to confine myself within the limits of time in which the story is laid. It is necessary, in order to excite interest, that the subject should be as it were translated, into the manners, customs and language of the day in which the reader lives". It is sufficient if the author succeeds in introducing nothing that is inconsistent with the age and its manners. The spirit is more important than the letter.

Bolt disregards anachronisms—of style and subject-matter. But that is only in order to enable him to communicate more freely with modern audiences. He scorns the time-honoured device of historical playwrights—a private language meant to indicate remoteness of time; there are no *gadzooks, zounds,* "by my halidom", and similar resurrections of times gone by. ("It is 1960 which I would clearly indicate to occupy the stage".) Shakespeare was full of anachronisms because he just did not bother about them, but Bolt admits them deliberately. Up to recent years anachronism was avoided on the stage and correctness of detail in local colour was insisted upon, and Bolt's attitude is thus in many respects a throw-back to older theatrical practice. He brings into service the language of all times, according to the mood of the moment, as he feels that he wants a sixteenth-century flavour or a smack of 1960. By the side of "forthink", "wit", and "nice" in their old senses, "easel and gall", one is startled by the everyday language of TV—"some decent clothes", "police work", "like a bat in a Sunday School" etc., and even an Americanism not familiar in English—"the case rests". At other times sixteenth-century words are used in their modern sense (*e.g.* "publican" and "pilot") and other later additions over the centuries are introduced, *e.g.* "acrobat".

There are no fictitious or imaginary characters in this play. Unlike many other dramatists, Bolt found all the material necessary in authentic characters, without the addition of specially invented characters. It is but a step from that to the use of passages actually uttered by More in real life. "My concern was to match these as best I could so that the theft should not be too obvious."

Critical Analysis of *A Man For All Seasons*

ACT I • SCENE I

Sir Thomas More and Richard Rich, a Young Man of Ambition, Converse Earnestly

The action of the play opens in the residence of Sir Thomas More at Chelsea. Sir Thomas is discovered in conversation with Richard Rich, an ambitious but impoverished young man. Rich is maintaining that every man has his price, whether it take the form of money, pleasure, honours, women or, as he terms it "bricks-and-mortar". The older man gently but firmly denies Rich's contention, which he considers childish. Rich then asserts that some men may even be bought by suffering. This proposition seems to interest More, who apparently takes the young man to mean that the prospect of suffering, in the sense of being tempted by martyrdom, may prove attractive to men of a certain kind. However, Rich is not being so subtle as the other imagines. He quickly goes on to say that he was thinking of the imposition of suffering, followed by the offer of escape, adding that it resolves itself in the practical question of how to make a man suffer sufficiently. This causes More to suspect that the younger man has been reading Machiavelli. In response to Sir Thomas' gentle but insistent questioning, Rich laughs a trifle self-consciously, but at length admits to the fact, saying that he did so on the advice of Thomas Cromwell. Both men agree as to Cromwell's ability, Rich adding that Cromwell has promised to "do something" for him. Sir Thomas expressing surprise that Rich is acquainted with Cromwell, the younger man goes on to complain that his talents are not being put to use. He protests bitterly that for seven months past he has been trying to gain an audience with Cardinal Wolsey, presumably with the object of securing a government appointment. After some further conversation, Sir Thomas tells Rich that the Dean of St. Paul's has offered him a position as a teacher, and advises him to take it since, as he says, "A man should go where he won't be tempted." Rich is evidently disappointed. Impulsively, Sir Thomas then hands Rich a beautiful Italian silver cup, asks him if he would like it, and if so what he will do with it. Rich appears surprised and confused; however, he gratefully accepts the gift, telling the other man that he will sell it, adding vehemently that he will buy some decent clothes with the proceeds. More goes on to tell Rich that the cup was a bribe, sent to him by a woman who subsequently brought a lawsuit before the Court of Requests. He adds that in public life bribery and corruption are commonplace, and urges Rich once again to accept the teaching post. Rich is inclined to be scornful, since he appears to seek public fame, rather than the obscurity of a teacher's life. Moreover, he evidently finds it difficult to believe Sir Thomas' assertion that he did not seek public life, but that it was inflicted upon him by royal command.

More's Family and The Duke of Norfolk Are Made Known To Us

While More and Rich are still in conversation, the Duke of Norfolk enters, followed closely by Lady Alice, More's wife, and Lady Margaret, his daughter. Norfolk and Lady Alice are involved in an emotional discussion about falconry. The Duke asserts that he recently saw a falcon swoop down from the clouds, a suggestion which Lady Alice denies as being impossible. Asked his opinion of the matter, More is somewhat noncommittal. The Duke goes on to say that if Lady Alice could ride, he would prove to her that he is right. The lady is indignant at the suggestion that she cannot ride, and proceeds to make a wager of thirty shillings that if she does go riding with the Duke, he will be unable to prove his assertion. Lady Alice becomes even more indignant when her husband suggests that she should not think of going riding with members of the nobility, since she is not, she protests, a mere "City Wife". More then blandly changes the subject, and asks Rich to clarify a somewhat pontifical remark that he has made concerning Aristotle's opinion of the difference between cloud and mist. From the ensuing conversation it appears that Norfolk sees little practical in Aristotle, and regards the doctrines of Machiavelli as unpleasant, although he has no first-hand knowledge of them. But Lady Margaret has read Machiavelli, and she tells the Duke mischievously that the Italian's ideas are, however, practical. Rich, concerned to make an impression on the noble visitor, speaks of Thomas Cromwell's opinions in the matter. The Duke is somewhat impressed to learn that Rich is acquainted with Cromwell, especially since this man, as he now tells the others, has been appointed Secretary to Cardinal Wolsey, the Lord Chancellor, within the past few days. More and his family are uneasy at the news, while Rich, by contrast, tells them that he likes Cromwell.

More is Summoned away by Wolsey to Hampton Court

Just as they are speaking of Cromwell, a steward enters with a letter, in which More is summoned to attend on Cardinal Wolsey concerning a matter of "the King's business". Before his departure More draws Norfolk's attention to the fact that Rich is desperately seeking employment, and the two latter leave together, but not before More has taken the opportunity once again to advise the young man to become a teacher. When only the steward remains, Rich returns by himself to retrieve the silver goblet.

ACT I • SCENE 2

Wolsey Tries, Unsuccessfully, To Gain Support for the King's Divorce

At Hampton Court, Wolsey is busy writing a "Latin Despatch". This is evidently a letter addressed to the Pope requesting a declaration to the effect that the King's marriage to Catherine of Aragon was invalid, or to set up a commission to decide the question. More having entered, the Lord Chancellor hands him the despatch to read. Asked his opinion of it, More at first hedges and merely concedes that it is well phrased. Pressed for his views, the visitor tells Wolsey that, in his opinion, the document ought to be shown to the King's Council before it is sent to Rome. Wolsey disagrees, mocks the other for his "moral squint", and asks him if he intends to be helpful. A distant trumpet call sounding, Wolsey and More go to the window together. According to Wolsey the King is at that very moment returning from visiting Anne Boleyn. He continues by telling More that Henry is determined to divorce Catherine because she has borne him no son, and that he wishes to marry Anne Boleyn, with the object of fathering a male heir so as to ensure the continuance of the Tudor dynasty. In spite of Wolsey's fierce and even violent pleas, More finds himself unable to promise support for the King's proposed divorce and subsequent re-marriage. Wolsey is greatly disturbed at More's expressed conviction that statesmen should not forsake their conscientious scruples in the pursuance of their public duties. The Lord Chancellor ridicules More's notions as to the efficiency of prayer, unless it be reinforced by positive action, and his contention that the country might well be governed by one of unswerving faith. He expresses doubt to More as to who will succeed to the Lord Chancellorship. When it is suggested that Cromwell may possibly succeed to the Lord Chancellorship, More is shocked, and admits that he would prefer to accept the burden himself. The scene ends when More, in a clever response, chides Wolsey for his worldliness, despite the fact that he is a Churchman.

ACT I • SCENE 3

Cromwell Appears, in Search of Information

On the Thames-side near Richmond, More seeks a river-boat to take him back to Chelsea. Having found one, he is talking to the boatman when Cromwell appears from behind an arch. The newcomer proceeds to criticize the boatman concerning his licence and the fares that he charges, and then pretends to recognise Sir Thomas. He announces that he is on his way to see Cardinal Wolsey, and asks More whether the Lord Chancellor was in a laughing mood when he left. More having replied in the negative, Cromwell expresses his regrets, assures the other that he is one of his many admirers, and leaves rather furtively.

Chapuys Appears, in Search of Information

More is walking down the wharf towards his boat, when Chapuys, the ambassador of Charles V, the Holy Roman Emperor, appears from behind another archway. Like Cromwell, he is in search of information, being apparently aware of More's visit to Wolsey. He tells Sir Thomas that his master, Charles V, who is the nephew of Catherine of Aragon, would feel himself insulted, should any insult be offered to his aunt. More makes no significant comment, and in response to further questions, refuses to remark further except to say that he and Wolsey parted on friendly terms. Chapuys appears to glean much from More's silence, and departs, having remarked that "A nod is as good as a wink to a blind horse". More finally gets into the waiting boat and is rowed back to his home at Chelsea.

ACT I • SCENE 4
Roper Pays Court to Lady Margaret But Leaves Distressed

Having arrived home from Richmond, More is told by his steward that his wife has retired, but that Lady Margaret is still up. The latter then enters, accompanied by William Roper, her suitor. More having commented that it is early morning, Roper replies that he has not come for breakfast, Lady Margaret adding that Roper wants to marry her. More says that this is impossible, but congratulates the young man when he announces that he has been called to the Bar. He assures Roper that there is nothing wrong with his family, but that there can be no question of his marrying his daughter so long as he is a heretic. Roper protests bitterly, and talks at some length of the shortcomings of the Church. But More is not to be swayed, and expresses the hope that eventually Roper will see his error, and return to the fold, when presumably he will be eligible to marry his daughter. The young man is then offered the use of one of the horses of the household and is rather pointedly told to go home. After Roper's departure, More reiterates that he will not permit him to marry Margaret as long as he is a heretic. Both Lady Margaret and her mother (who enters shortly after the visitor has left) are anxious to know the purpose of More's conversation with Wolsey, but he will tell them nothing beyond the simple fact that the Cardinal required him to read a Latin Dispatch. Lady Alice then reveals that, after More's departure for Richmond, Norfolk had mentioned her husband's name as possible successor to Wolsey. Sir Thomas makes it clear to the ladies that he does not seek the Lord Chancellorship, and that he doubts whether the office will become vacant so long as Cardinal Wolsey is alive.

ACT I • SCENE 5
Cromwell and Chapuys Reveal Their Continued Thirst for Information

As the scene opens, at Hampton Court Palace, Cromwell and Rich are seen to encounter each other. It appears that Rich is now librarian to the Duke of Norfolk, while Cromwell is in King Henry's personal service, in the capacity of what he describes as "The King's Ear." Cromwell teases

Rich by telling him that he is in a comparative backwater, in spite of the fact that More, now Lord Chancellor, in succession to Wolsey, is an old friend of his. Rich, for his part is curious to know what Cromwell's office entails. Chapuys entering, Cromwell introduces him to Rich. Like Rich, the Ambassador is curious to know something of the other's exact relationship to the King. Cromwell tells them that, as distinct from Justices, Chancellors, Admirals and the like, whose duties are constitutional, he is concerned with getting things done. He talks at some length of the imminent launching of the "Great Harry" at Deptford, and mentions some of the details with which he had been personally concerned, adding that he is stocking his mind in preparation for "higher things". Cromwell is disturbed when Chapuys corrects him concerning the armament of the "Great Harry", and then hints of the King's impending visit to Chelsea to persuade Sir Thomas More to agree to his divorce. Cromwell admits that he will not be present, but apparently believes that More may be prevailed upon to change his mind. At this point More's household steward enters, and is recognized as such by Chapuys, who then reluctantly takes his leave, but remains within earshot. Cromwell, who has apparently sent for More's steward, questions him about his master's habits, and learns that, although the new Lord Chancellor does not discuss the King's divorce with his wife and daughter, he appears worried and ill-at-ease, and goes pale when the matter is even mentioned. Cromwell gives the steward a coin and waves him away. He and Rich then leave together, the former protesting that he has no information to give him. Left to himself, More's steward is joined by Chapuys and his attendant. The Ambassador proceeds to question the steward closely as to More's religious habits, of which he receives satisfactory assurances. The steward admits that Cromwell, too, has been seeking information about his master. Chapuys rewards him and then departs, whereupon Rich re-enters, presumably at Cromwell's behest. Giving the steward a coin, Rich asks him what Chapuys wanted, and is given a truthful, if somewhat impertinent answer. The steward then pointedly indicates the direction taken by Cromwell. After rebuking the other furiously for his insolence, Rich departs, leaving the steward to reflect alone.

ACT I • SCENE 6
Sir Thomas More is the Cause of Acute Domestic Distress

The scene opens at More's house at Chelsea, where the King is expected to arrive at any moment. Lady Alice, Lady Margaret and the Duke of Norfolk are greatly disturbed since Sir Thomas is nowhere to be found. They all protest and at length question the steward, who seems as much at a loss as they. A royal fanfare sounding at no great distance away, everyone present becomes even more distracted, since there is still no sign of More. However, the Lord Chancellor suddenly appears, dressed in a cassock. He is entirely at ease, and tells the others that he has just returned from Vespers. It is brought to his notice that he is somewhat neglectful, and that he is improperly dressed for the occasion. He is then forcibly deprived of his cassock, and is made presentable, although it appears that he is still wearing his second best stockings.

The King Reveals His Ability in Several Fields of Endeavour

The King, in the guise of a ship's pilot, wearing cloth of gold, then enters, blowing his whistle softly. He is greeted courteously by Sir Thomas, who introduces him to his wife and daughter. Henry appears impressed by Lady Margaret, who is something of a bluestocking, and they converse in Latin for a moment or two. However, he is somewhat displeased, since it is evident that her Latin is better than his. The King then quotes from the bible to the effect that books and bookishness may be taken to extreme lengths. Recovering his good humour, he asks Lady Margaret if she can dance. When she admits that she cannot, he responds by asserting that he dances superbly, and displays his calf proudly, as though to prove the point. The King goes on to point mockingly at Norfolk, adding that, although the Duke has the legs of a wrestler, he is nevertheless capable of throwing him. He then seizes the embarassed Norfolk, and asks Lady Margaret if he should display his ability. When she replies in the negative, Henry remarks that she is gentle, and that she shall read to him. Having accepted his hostess' invitation to stay to supper, the King, evidently still much impressed by Lady Margaret, blurts out that he is something of a scholar. The young lady responds graciously by praising his well-known work, in which he upheld the seven Sacraments of the Church, whereupon Henry admits that he received some help from her father. As Norfolk and the ladies are about to withdraw, Henry asks Lady Margaret if she likes music. She replies that she does. The King then offers her his whistle, and asks her to blow it. When she does so, stately and somewhat cloying music is heard outside, which gradually recedes, as the royal barge moves out of earshot. The rest having been finally dismissed, King Henry and Sir Thomas are left together.

King Henry Tries, Unsuccessfully, to Win More's Support for His Divorce

Henry appears to be in a thoughtful mood, and is seemingly entranced by the sound of the music outside, which gradually becomes fainter. He tells More that only that day he has launched his new ship, the "Great Harry", and that he has actually steered her under sail. The King goes on to express regret that he must continue to live in the indecent atmosphere of the Court, when, as he says, "he has friends with gardens". Even more insincerely, he tells More that he regards him as his friend, and hopes that he is readier to prove his friendship than he was to become Lord Chancellor. More appears surprised when told that he was nominated as Lord Chancellor by Wolsey himself, but irritates the King by venturing the opinion that the late Cardinal was a man of incomparable ability. Henry then complains about Wolsey's alleged villainy and pride, asserting that he had even wished to become Pope. At this juncture, he breaks off to talk proudly of the "Great Harry", and the way that he handled her. The King, in a somewhat casual manner, then comes to the point, and asks More whether he has thought any more of his intended divorce. In evident distress. More answers that he has, but that he sees his own attitude so clearly, that he would wish to dismiss it from his mind. Henry responds by saying that the other cannot have considered the matter sufficiently, and expresses deep concern and regret that More should wish to deny him what he desires above all else. Sir Thomas then exposes his right arm, and assures the King that he would willingly sacrifice it to him, if by that means he might be persuaded to agree to his sovereign's point of view. More then asks the King's pardon, and takes leave to remind him that when he accepted the Lord Chancellorship, Henry had promised not to pursue the matter. The King is momentarily enraged, but quickly regains his composure. There follows a brief exchange, during which the King claims biblical authority (Leviticus 18-16) in support of his contention that his marriage to Catherine was illegal, while More, for his part, asserts that the marriage was legal, and quotes Deuteronomy 25-5 to prove his point. The King counters More's argument by contending that Deuteronomy is ambiguous, to which the other replies that he is not fit to meddle in such matters, and that it would be better to consult the Holy See. In a tone of reproof, Henry asks if a man needs a Pope to tell him when he has sinned, and goes on to say that he admits his sin and duly repents of it, notwithstanding which, God continues to punish him by denying him a son and heir. Warming to his subject, he declares it to be his duty to divorce the Queen, even in the face of Papal opposition. In view of the King's determination to proceed with his divorce, More is at a loss to understand why his approval is sought, and, in response to his further question, is assured by the King that it is because, in opposition to many others, he is an honest man and is known to be honest. After a further expression of regret by More, the conversation becomes rambling. The two discuss music for a moment or two, and the King reveals his authorship of the air which had captivated them a short time before. More repeats his invitation for Henry to remain to dinner, but the King replies in a somewhat non-committal manner, and it seems that he has become moody again. Then, to More's evident surprise, Henry bursts out violently that he will tolerate no opposition in the manner of the divorce. He reminds the other that he is the Lord Chancellor, and that he does not take kindly to his attitude, although he promises to disregard it. More listens patiently, and the King proceeds to lose his temper completely, speaking in viciously contemptuous terms of the Pope and the Princes of the Church. He ends his tirade by warning More again that he will tolerate no opposition whatsoever to his designs. More is obviously distressed by the King's outburst, and stresses that he is a loyal minister of the crown. He is about to hint that he is prepared to resign, when Henry interrupts him, urging that the priests who oppose him are liars and traitors. More asks rhetorically, but in an unsteady tone of voice, whether he is a babbler, and the King replies that he is stubborn, but that there is no man whom he would prefer to raise to a position of outstanding eminence. At this point there is a chiming of bells, indicating that it is eight o'clock. The King then suggests that they have supper, but apparently recalling the time, decides that he had better go, because of the imminent change of tide. Lady Alice having reappeared, Henry apologises to her for not staying, and takes his leave.

More's Family is Uneasy About the Future

After the King's departure, Lady Alice shows herself to be most anxious. She appeals to her husband to remain on friendly terms with the King. More makes light of the matter, and concludes by telling her that he is not of the stuff of which martyrs are made. He is somewhat put out when Roper appears, followed by Lady Margaret. It appears that Roper has experienced a change of heart. He is no longer a heretic, one gathers. While admitting the corruption that exists within the body of the Church, he considers that the Church itself is sacrosanct, and that any attack made upon it constitutes an attack on God. Having announced that he has been offered a seat in the next Parliament, Roper speaks so emotionally that he embarrasses More, who reminds him that, as a Minister of the Crown, there are certain things that he may not hear. Roper then declares that the Court has succeeded in corrupting More, a remark which annoys Lady Alice intensely. At this point Rich is announced, and is introduced to Roper. The newcomer is evidently ill at ease, and appears to sense an atmosphere of hostility. As though to re-establish his good name, he tells More that Cromwell is asking questions about him. Pointing to Matthew, More's steward, Rich asserts that he is one of Cromwell's sources of information, adding that Chapuys is collecting information also. More is grave, but unruffled, at these revelations, but remarks on Rich's nervous manner. Rich then implores Sir Thomas to give him employment, stressing that he would be steadfast. The rest watch him fixedly, as he makes his departure. There is a general outburst after Rich has left, Roper and the two ladies sharing the impression that Rich is an evil man, whose activities should be curtailed. More, however, refuses to take any action whatsoever against Rich on the grounds that he has committed no crime, and is therefore beyond the jurisdiction of the law. This attitude provokes an outburst from Roper to the effect that More displays undue respect for the law, and regards it as his god. There follow some bitter remarks, More asserting that his only god is God. He goes on to criticize Roper's facility to change his opinions, and to make everyone aware of them. Adding that, in the last resort, he will be sheltered by the law, More leaves somewhat huffily. Sensing that there is something seriously wrong, Roper questions the two ladies, and Lady Alice tells him that, since the matter of the King's divorce was raised, her husband has been quiet and restrained. More reappears shortly afterwards, apologises to Roper for his harshness, and pays tribute to the other's high principles. The others try to draw him out, but More will vouchsafe them nothing beyond assuring him that he has not disobeyed the King, that he considers himself entirely safe, and that all public figures are subject to the kind of inquiries which Cromwell is apparently pursuing. The three then leave for the dining room to partake of the "simple supper", with which they had hoped to honour King Henry.

ACT I • SCENE 7

Rich is Rewarded for Services Rendered

Cromwell appears in a public house. He is apparently concerned to find a secluded corner, since he carries on to the publican to this effect. He admits to Rich, who joins him shortly afterwards, that he is a little drunk. But, as he tells his companion, he is drunk, not with alcohol, but with success. In response to Rich's questioning, Cromwell finally admits that he has been appointed Secretary to the King's Council. He is at pains to tell Rich that the confidential information that he has just imparted is evidence of the fact that he imposes some trust in him. Rich hastily adds that he would never repeat such matters, whereupon Cromwell asks him what sort of matters he would repeat. After some discussion, Rich admits that it would depend on what he was offered for the information. Cromwell then offers the other his congratulations on having been appointed Collector of Revenues for the Diocese of York. Rich, rather sceptically, asks Cromwell if he is empowered to offer him the appointment. Assured by Cromwell that he is, Rich asks what he must do to be so honoured. Cromwell, pacing up and down, insists that there are no rules. He then goes on to explain what he calls the "factor of convenience" in public life, and tells his companion that if the King is determined to have his divorce, then it is the duty of "administrators" to make this possible. Rich is evidently somewhat apprehensive, not knowing what may be required of him, a fact which prompts him to remark that he has lost his innocence. Cromwell continues by saying that the difficulty in the way of the King's divorce is the Pope, and that Sir Thomas More unfortunately entertains some rather fixed ideas in the matter of Papal authority. The older man then asks the other how much he got for the silver goblet that More once gave him. Rich gives a truthful answer, and, in response to further questioning, tells Cromwell that it had been given to More as a bribe by a woman litigant, and that he can remember the shop where he sold it. Having said all this, the young man appears uneasy, and asks Cromwell what use is made of the information that he collects. Cromwell at first replies by saying that such "tid-bits" are rarely made use of, but afterwards admits to Rich that those "upright, steadfast men" who oppose the course of events are likely to be fit only for Heaven. He then asserts that More is a sensible man, whom it is possible to frighten, upon which Rich protests that he is an "innocent". Cromwell cuts short the discussion and starts to leave, when Rich (evidently upset) shouts after him saying that he has mistaken his man, and that More is incapable of being frightened. This statement infuriates Cromwell, who promptly returns and holds Rich's finger in the flame of a candle for a moment, remarking, as he does so, that one who does not know fright has never been burnt. Rich cries out at the pain, and is horrified at the fact that Cromwell appears to have enjoyed his brief role as a torturer.

ACT II • SCENE I

More is taken to task by Roper, now a devout Catholic

More and Roper, now his son-in-law, are revealed at the former's house at Chelsea. Roper is attired in black and is wearing a cross, a fact which excites More's criticism. In reply to the other's remarks, Roper contends that the time has come when men should declare their allegiance. More is quizzical, and tells Roper that he looks like a Spaniard, adding that he would not have lasted six months in Spain during his heretical period. The younger man then points to More's chain of office, telling him that he is lowering himself by wearing it. More replies by saying that there is nothing degrading in it, since men greater than he have worn it. It appears that Sir Thomas has made up his mind to resign the Lord Chancellorship, should it happen that the Bishops then in Convocation at Canterbury will submit to the demand of the King, and acknowledge him as the Supreme Head of the Church in England. Roper is cynical when More reminds him of this, and hints that the Church is already subject to the Palace, and the King is its Supreme Head. More insists that this is not so, and that the proposed Act of Parliament contains the important qualification - "so far as the law of God allows". Roper, wishing to pursue the argument, is silenced by his father-in-law, who reminds him that he now has a wife, and should therefore be discreet.

Chapuys Joins Them, Anxious to Know More's Views

Lady Margaret, who has just joined the other, then announces that Chapuys has arrived. The latter enters, interrupting the conversation. Adopting an insincere religious pose, he tells More that he is not free from some suspicion of saintliness. More is not pleased by the implications of this remark, and asks the Ambassador what he wants of him. Chapuys protests that he does not really want anything, whereupon More, realising that he may have something confidential to impart, dismisses Roper and Lady Margaret. Left alone, Chapuys comes to the point. He proceeds to tell More in forthright fashion that he cannot believe that he will allow himself to be associated with King Henry's recent actions in connection with Queen Catherine. More replies that, willy-nilly, subjects are associated with the actions of kings, and that another Lord Chancellor might have done worse than he. Chapuys then goes on to remark that there is a rumour to the effect that if the Church in Convocation submits to the King, the other will resign, adding that if he should do so, the fact would be applauded by half the population. More looks sceptical at this latter remark, when Chapuys qualifies it by telling him that he has recently returned from the north of England where the people appear ripe for revolt.

More Gives up His Public Office and Resigns Himself to Obscurity

Roper then enters excitedly, followed by Norfolk and the two ladies. Chapuys makes an excuse, pretends to leave, but hovers in the background. Norfolk interrupts Roper to tell More that the Bishops in Convocation have submitted to the King's demands, and that "the connection with Rome" has been severed. It appears that only Bishop Fisher has disagreed, a circumstance which evokes More's admiration. At this juncture, it is noticed that Chapuys is still within earshot, and all turn to watch him as he makes his exit. More then begins to divest himself of his chain of office, Lady Margaret finally helping him. As he does so, he is criticized both by Lady Alice and Norfolk. More declares hotly that what has happened is not "Reformation" but war against the Church itself. He declines to say whether he believes that Catherine is, in fact, the King's wife or not, except to the King himself, and in private. He continues that, while admitting to the Pope's shortcomings, he believes the Pontiff to be the Vicar of Christ on earth. Norfolk interrupts him to say that he is risking everything for a theory, a remark which More counters by saying that, theory or not, *he* believes it. Having received Norfolk's assurance that he is speaking in confidence, and that he would respect his promise, even if the King should order him to repeat what he had said, More then suggests rhetorically that Norfolk would be guilty of disloyalty to his sovereign by so doing. Norfolk is naturally indignant at this turn of conversation, which More justifies by admitting to the other that he is afraid. He is reassured, however, by Norfolk, who tells him that, much as the King dislikes the fact of his resignation, he will bear in mind his past services. As Norfolk is about to take his leave, More tells him of Chapuys' remarks concerning his recent tour of northern England, adding that he shares the Ambassador's view that there will possibly be trouble there. He apparently thinks that this will come about because of the strength of the Roman Catholic Church in those parts, and adds the further warning that the Old Alliance (that between Scotland and France) may prove a further cause of strife. Norfolk reassures him, saying that Chapuys was accompanied on his recent tour by one of Cromwell's agents. More is provoked to an angry retort when Norfolk, in the act of leaving, remarks sarcastically that he is glad to know that the other retains some appearance of patriotism. More does his best to justify his action to his family. Roper appears to be the most understanding, while Lady Alice, apprehensive of the future, not only takes her husband to task, but her son-in-law also. She seems to think that he will not be allowed to retire peacefully into obscurity, although More appears convinced that he will not be molested, provided that they refrain from discussing the question of the King's Supremacy, and the matter of his divorce. He enjoins her to bear witness that he has never made any statement on these matters, to which she assents. The steward then enters, saying that the rest of the servants wish to know what has happened.

More replies that most of them will have to be dismissed, but that he will find new places for them all. He adds that the household will be a smaller one, and asks the steward whether he will be content to remain at a lower wage. Matthew, however, regretfully declines to do so.

ACT II • SCENE 2
Cromwell is Concerned that More Should Declare His Support of The King

At Hampton Court Palace, Cromwell and Norfolk are discussing the former Lord Chancellor; Norfolk argues that, since More is maintaining silence, he should be left unmolested. Cromwell then comments that if More reported Chapuys' remarks about the probability of an uprising in the North, this fact would suggest that he is hostile to Spain, and is therefore a supporter of the English Government. Norfolk agrees that although More may be something of a crank, he is no traitor, and for that reason should remain undisturbed. Cromwell believes that, with a little pressure, More may be made to affirm his loyalty to the "present administration". Norfolk, however, is not convinced, and says so, whereupon Cromwell remarks that the King himself does not agree to "let sleeping dogs lie". He then goes on to say that there is evidence that More accepted bribes during the period of his judicature, an assertion which provokes a disbelieving protest from Norfolk. Cromwell thereupon rings a bell, and Rich enters, accompanied by a woman, Catherine Anger. In response to questioning, the woman attests that she was once a party in a property case brought before the Court of Requests, and that she sent Sir Thomas the gift of an Italian silver cup, which he accepted. Her evidence is supported by Rich, who states that the cup was given to him by More. Norfolk is able to recall the incident, since he was at More's house when Rich left with it in his possession. However, the Duke regards the matter somewhat lightly, saying that the moment More realized the cup was a bribe, he got rid of it. Cromwell agrees that the facts will bear this interpretation, but adds that if this charge fails, "something better" will be found. Norfolk, having protested that he wishes no part in this conspiracy against More, Cromwell tells him that he has no choice, because the King wishes him to be active in the matter, and that if he is not, the fact of his known friendship for the other may lead him into trouble. Norfolk, realizing that he is being threatened, is furious, and leaves abruptly. Left to themselves Cromwell and Rich discuss the matter briefly. They appear to think that it may be difficult to force More into agreement, Cromwell suggesting that, since he is such, "a slippery fish", a net of a finer mesh is needed, which he and Rich will forthwith proceed to weave. Cromwell having taken his departure, More's former steward enters and offers Rich his services. The young man admits that his household "is expanding", and appears to accept Matthew's offer, adding shrilly that he remembers the other to have been rather disrespectful in the past. However, he appears somewhat mollified when Matthew assures him that matters will be different henceforth, now that he is beginning to "make his way in the world". Rich having departed, the steward follows him, carrying the other's papers and remarking quietly that he is quite capable of "managing" his new master.

ACT II • SCENE 3

Chapuys Brings More a Letter From His Master Which The Other Refuses to Accept

Chapuys and his attendant arrive at More's house at Chelsea, where they are received by Lady Alice. As they wait for More to appear, they discuss the implications of More's apparent hostility towards Cromwell, which they construe as being favourable to their master, King Charles. When More enters, he demands to know of Chapuys whether his visit is official or otherwise. After some little discussion, Chapuys admits that he has brought Sir Thomas a letter from King Charles, which he proceeds to offer him. More, however, refuses even to touch it. Chapuys then tells the other that the letter has nothing to do with affairs of State, but simply expresses King Charles' admiration of the attitude displayed by More and Fisher in the matter of Henry's divorce from Catherine of Aragon. More protests that he has taken no stand in this connection, and adds irritably that it might be a difficult matter to persuade King Henry that such a letter was not, in fact, "an affair of State". Chapuys then assures More that he has taken extreme care in coming to see him, mentioning that his visit is "very much incognito". More, however, cuts him short, telling him that it is not a question of what precautions the Ambassador has taken, but of his own duty, which would be to take the letter immediately to the King. Chapuys is evidently flabbergasted having regard to what he understands are More's views on the matter, but the latter sternly remarks that while his views are seemingly taken for granted, his loyalty appears to be in question. At this point Lady Margaret and Lady Alice enter. The former is carrying bracken that she has collected for burning. Having made a brief comment to his wife on the dryness of the fuel, More shows the two ladies Chapuy's letter, and asks them to witness the fact that it is unopened, and that the seal is still intact. He then tells Chapuys, pointedly, that he regrets that he cannot ask him to stay, adding, as evidence of his poverty, that the bracken fire is considered to be a luxury. Chapuys and his attendant then withdraw, the former remarking as he leaves that his master's admiration of More will not be diminished. Left to themselves More and the two ladies discuss domestic matters. It appears that a group of the clergy of all ranks have recently raised the sum of four thousand pounds, and offered it to More as a gift. He has declined it, however, on the grounds that his acceptance of it might be construed as a reward for his refusal to approve of the King's divorce, and could conceivably prove dangerous. His wife and daughter, particularly the former, are resentful of their poverty, and try, without success, to persuade him to change his mind. But, much as he sympathises with them, he cannot bring himself to agree, arguing that his stand on this matter is governed by considerations of safety. Ironically, they are interrupted by Roper, who tells More that a messenger has just arrived from Hampton Court, summoning him before Cromwell "to answer certain charges". Lady Alice is evidently distressed, while Lady Margaret pleads, unsuccessfully, to accompany her father. More makes light of the matter, asserting that Cromwell is not to be feared, since he believes his case to be watertight.

ACT II • SCENE 4
More is Interrogated by Cromwell at Hampton Court

At Hampton Court Palace, Cromwell interrogates More, while Rich acts as secretary. Cromwell's manner is friendly and informal, despite which More demands to know the charges against him. More's inquisitor assures him that there are no charges as such, but that he wishes to clarify what he terms "certain ambiguities of behaviour". Cromwell adds that he is amazed at the fact that More, once prominent in public life, has so much retired from it, and appears to be in opposition to "the whole movement of the times". More makes a non-committal reply, to which Cromwell responds by stating that the King is not pleased with him, but that even now, if More will agree to align himself with the Universities, the Bishops, and Parliament, there is no honour that he might be denied. Again More shows no sign that he might be willing to change his mind. Cromwell's manner then changes, and he goes on to talk about the matter of the "Holy Maid of Kent", who was executed for making certain prophecies concerning the King. More admits that he knew the woman, whom he sympathized with, but contends that she was ignorant, misguided, and possibly mentally unbalanced. On further questioning, More admits that he actually met the woman and wrote to her, but that she was not guilty of treason, and that he advised her not to meddle in matters concerning King and State. He adds that he can prove the truth of this last point, since he took the precaution to keep a copy of his letter to her, which was duly witnessed. Commenting on More's caution, Cromwell changes the subject, and then adds that there is a more serious charge concerning a theological work, "A Defence of the Seven Sacraments", for which its author, the King, had been given by the Pope the title of "Defender of the Faith". It is contended by Cromwell that More actually wrote the book, but the other vows that he merely answered certain questions concerning it, that were put to him by the King, and that it was essentially the King's own project. Cromwell then asks More if he has any statement to make in the matter of the King's marriage to Anne Boleyn. More replies that he understood that he would not be asked this question again. When Cromwell straightens him out on this notion, More answers his inquisitor by saying that his implied threats are "terrors for children", and that he is unafraid. As More is about to leave, Cromwell tells him that the King regards his attitude as ungrateful, villainous and traitorous. Rich enters after More's departure, asking whether Cromwell still believes that Sir Thomas can be frightened. Cromwell answers ominously that either More will give his blessing to the King's marriage, or he will be destroyed.

ACT II • SCENE 5
More Deliberately Insults Norfolk With a View To Ending Their Friendship

More appears at the river-side, calling for a boat. Norfolk then enters, and More complains to him that he is experiencing difficulty —even with boatmen. The Duke tells him that the boatmen cannot be blamed for their reluctance to take him home. There follows a long argument between the two men. Norfolk tells More that he is acting foolishly, and that even if he is not concerned for himself, he should consider his friends. Each asserts his friendship for the other, but More makes it clear that, even though Norfolk may be used by the King to encompass his ruin, he will not be shaken in his attitude. Norfolk having reasserted his friendship for the other, More deliberately insults him by criticizing the aristocracy in general, and casting doubt on Norfolk's personal honour. In spite of himself, the Duke responds angrily, and attempts to strike More, who avoids his blow. Lady Margaret, entering at the climax of the quarrel followed by Roper, is told by her father that the man she had seen departing was the Duke. The newcomers then tell More that a new Act of Parliament has been passed concerning an oath to be taken in the matter of the royal marriage. More tries to make light of the matter, saying that they should hurry home to examine the terms of the new enactment. In response to Lady Margaret's question, More will admit nothing of his disagreement with Norfolk, except to say that he spoke slightingly of water spaniels. He then adds that only by examining the terms of the recent Act of Parliament will it be possible to determine how to evade its consequences.

ACT II • SCENE 6
More, Now a Prisoner, Appears Before the Seventh Commission at the Tower

By this time, More is a prisoner in the Tower of London. As the scene opens he is about to appear before the Seventh Commission, consisting of Thomas Cromwell, the Duke of Norfolk and Thomas Cranmer, Archbishop of Canterbury. The accused man is shown a copy of the Act of Succession, and a list of those who have sworn to it. On being asked to swear likewise, More refuses to do so. He is then asked if he will recognise the offspring of Anne Boleyn as the King's heirs, to which he readily assents. The question then arises as to why More will not take the oath previously asked of him, but he steadfastly refuses to state his reasons. More denies that his attitude is necessarily treasonable, and insists that, notwithstanding the eminence and honesty of those who have taken the necessary oath, he cannot conscientiously follow suit. Having then told the Commission that he will vouchsafe his reasons only to the King in person, he asks to leave. Cromwell having warned the prisoner that he does not seem to appreciate the seriousness of his position, there follows a wrangle in which the former is worsted. More, asking to be allowed more books, is told that he should not be permitted any at all, and Cromwell later gives orders thay they should be removed the next day. After requesting, without success, that he may see his family, More returns to his cell. When the prisoner has departed, his jailer is asked, but with negative result, whether he has ever heard More speak of the King's divorce and re-marriage, and his position as head of the Church. He then agrees to report anything that Sir Thomas may say of these matters to the Lieutenant of the Tower, and swears an oath to this effect. The jailer having departed, Norfolk protests to Cromwell that More is being harshly treated, and receives the reply that the King is becoming impatient. Left alone with Rich, who has been in attendance during the proceedings, Cromwell is asked by the young man if he may be considered for the vacant office of Attorney-General for Wales. The response, however, is one of furious impatience. Cromwell broods aloud, and toys with the mechanism of a rack, as though considering its use to force More's compliance. Finally, he mutters that the King would not permit it, and that a gentler way must be found. His change of tactics is evident from the fact that, in the succeeding scene, More is permitted to see his family.

ACT II • SCENE 7

More's Family Visit Him in the Tower

On a dull, grey morning, the jailer enters More's cell, telling him that his family has come to see him. More starts up in evident surprise that he is being allowed visitors, and then leaves his cell to meet his wife, daughter and son-in-law, who await him outside. He greets his family ecstatically, but Roper and the two ladies are so horrified by the surroundings, that they can think and speak of little else. After a moment or two, Margaret tells her father that they have brought him some gifts of food and wine. However, the atmosphere is seemingly still tense, and More makes an exclamation of bewilderment, as though to ask them to come to the point. Roper then announces that Lady Margaret has taken an oath to persuade More to change his attitude. There follows a discussion between More and his daughter. She argues that he should swear his support of the Act of Succession, even although he really thinks otherwise. But More is not to be shaken, despite the fact that Lady Margaret speaks beseechingly to him, and praises his many achievements in the interests of justice and truth. Lady Alice then interrupts angrily to ask whether he is content to remain in a pest-ridden prison, when he might be comfortably at home. More replies that if he could see a possible loop-hole, he would take advantage of it. He then asks Lady Margaret jestingly if she has any more tempting offers to make him, and she seizes the opportunity to tell him what a wretched time they are having at home in his absence. More responds somewhat bitterly to the effect that even the King does not torture him. At this stage the jailer enters briefly, saying that the visitors must go within the next two minutes. More then suggests that Roper should play dice with the jailer outside in an endeavour to prolong the interview. His son-in-law having left, More tells the two ladies that they should leave the country immediately, but by different routes. He goes on to say that he does not think he can be brought to trial, because his persecutors have no case to make. Lady Alice, however, is angry, and turns her back on him. There follows a violent discussion. She, for her part, does not appear to share her husband's optimism, and asserts that his death, which he can avoid should he wish, will not benefit her in any way. More is shocked, but pays a tribute to her honesty. His wife responds by telling him that she is afraid that after he is dead, she will hate his memory. The two then embrace emotionally, More trying to comfort her. Lady Alice then assures her husband that even if she does not understand him in the matter of the oath that he refuses to take, she appreciates full well that he is the best man she has ever met or is likely to meet. She adds for good measure that God does not seem to be giving them much help, and that if anyone wants her opinion of the King and his Council, she will willingly give it. More is greatly gratified at this evidence of his wife's spirit, and is apparently about to repeat his previous advice to them to leave the country, when Roper and the jailer re-enter, arguing fiercely. There follows a bitter wrangle between the turnkey and the rest, which is only resolved when the former threatens to call the guard, since, as he makes clear, More is closely watched. The visitors having taken their departure, the jailer apologizes to his prisoner for his desire to keep out of trouble.

ACT II • SCENE 8

At Westminster, More is Tried, Found Guilty and Sentenced to Death

More is revealed in the court-room, carrying a scroll, and being helped to a chair. There is a fanfare of trumpets, and the accused man rises as Norfolk and Cranmer enter. Norfolk begins the proceedings by announcing that More is charged with High Treason, but that even now he may be pardoned , should he be prepared to "forthink and repent of" his stubborn opinions. More responds by stating that he cannot conscientiously foreswear his honest convictions, and is then permitted to sit down. Cromwell, having been asked to read the charge, remarks before doing so, that it is the same in substance as that preferred against Bishop Fisher, who was executed that morning. The charge is then read out; it is to the effect that More "did conspire traitorously and maliciously to deny" the King his title as "Supreme Head of the Church of England". Surprised,

More denies the charge, but is told by Cromwell that he has refused to take an oath in support of the King's title. More protests that silence is not denial, adds that his silence has been punished by imprisonment, and that he therefore does not understand why he has been brought to trial. Norfolk reminds the accused man that he is charged with High Treason, whereupon Cromwell interrupts by hinting that the punishment for this offence is more serious than imprisonment. More, not slow to take the hint, tells the court that death must come to all, even to Kings. Cromwell affects to regard this as a treasonable remark, at which Norfolk tells More that the death of Kings is not in question. The accused man then having expressed the hope that his death is not in question either, unless he is found guilty, Norfolk assures him eagerly that his life is in his own hands, as it always has been.

In response to a direct question from Cromwell, More reiterates that his defence rests on his silence. Cromwell then addresses the jury at length. He contends that while silence, in certain circumstances, may mean nothing, it may also, according to the context in which it is maintained, have either a positive or negative significance. Cromwell then reminds the court that many of the King's subjects throughout the country have declared, on oath, that His Majesty's claim to the title of "Supreme Head" is just and valid. The fact, therefore, that More refuses to swear such an oath, is, he contends, tantamount to a denial of the King's claim to the title under dispute. More counters this argument in legalistic terms, saying that the accepted maxim is "Silence Gives Consent", and that the court should therefore construe his silence as evidence of consent. Cromwell having suggested that the public interpret More's silence in the opposite sense, he asks the other whether he pretends that he wishes it to be understood that he supports the King's position. More replies by saying that while the world must construe according to its wits, it is the duty of the court to construe according to the law. Cromwell then tells the court that More is trying to obscure the issue. There ensues a further argument, More protesting the impartiality of the law and man's loyalty to his conscience, while Cromwell is bitterly contemptuous, and speaks of patriotism. At length, Sir Richard Rich is called to give evidence. He testifies that during a recent conversation with More, the latter had said that he was unable to accept the King as Supreme Head of the Church, because Parliament was not competent to make a law to this effect. More denies the evidence of Rich, accuses him in forthright terms of perjury, and suggests it is most improbable that he would have made such an admission to a man like Rich. More then mentions the fact that, on the occasion of his supposed admission to Rich, two other men were present. Cromwell, however, states that these two men, Southwell and Palmer, are unfortunately absent "on the King's business", but that he has a statement from them to the effect that they did not overhear the conversation between More and Rich. The witness having been given permission to withdraw, More asks him as he leaves if he may examine his chain of office. Observing the design of a red dragon on the medallion, he requests an explanation. Cromwell tells him that Rich is now Attorney-General for Wales, whereupon More is unable to resist the jibe that while it profits a man nothing to give his soul for the world, it is even more questionable to do so for Wales. Rich having made his exit, Cromwell is about to tell More that even now it is not too late to recant, but is cut short by the accused man. Norfolk then instructs the jury to retire and consider its verdict, but Cromwell interrupts to suggest that, in view of the evidence, this procedure should not be necessary. In response to Norfolk's question, he is told by the Foreman that More has been found guilty. As the Duke is about to pass sentence, he is reminded by More that it is customary to ask a prisoner if he has anything to say before sentence is passed. Somewhat upset, Norfolk puts the question to him. More then states that he has taken every possible step to avoid his present situation, but that the court was determined to condemn him. Such being so, he continues, he will now state his views. More goes on to tell the court clearly and distinctly that, in his view, the Supremacy of the Church is a Spiritual Supremacy, and that the King in Parliament has no power to bestow it. He further asserts that the immunity of the Church is guaranteed both in Magna Carta and in the words of the King's Coronation Oath. More's statement evokes from Cromwell the comment that he has thereby proved himself to be malicious. The condemned man then makes some few brief comments in conclusion. He protests his loyalty to the King, maintains that he is not sorry to die, and adds, angrily and scornfully, that he has not been condemned in the matter of the King's Supremacy, but because he opposed his divorce and re-marriage. Finally, Norfolk pronounces sentence, that of death by beheading.

ACT II • SCENE 9

More Pays the Penalty of an Independent Spirit

The execution scene is short lived. More is accompanied part of the way to the scaffold by Norfolk, who offers him drink, but is declined. Lady Margaret takes an emotional farewell of her father, who tries to comfort her. More is then approached by Catherine Anger, who mocks him, but is quietly reproved. Finally, there is a brief exchange between the condemned man and Archbishop Cranmer, who appears to be envious of the other's self-control. Kneeling before the block, More removes his hat, having previously assured the executioner not to be afraid of his office. Darkness descends, and a moment later there is heard the cry "Behold-the head-of a traitor!" As the light is partially restored, Cromwell and Chapuys are observed to leave the scene together—arm in arm.

Notes on The Text

PROLOGUE

Big property basket - a large basket or hamper used to hold the smaller items of stage property needed in the play.

Common Man - the author tells us in his Preface that this character represents "that which is common to us all". The Common Man appears in various guises (More's steward, a boatman, a jailer, etc.) He is able, so to speak, to step out of the play and talk to the audience, explaining the action as he links the scenes together. His function in the play is indicated to some extent by the property basket and its contents.

Speaking costumes - clothes which suggest the rank and importance of the characters concerned.

Embroidered mouths - mouths capable of giving voice to more elaborate and refined speech than that which is characteristic of the Common Man.

Reduce Old Adam to the Common Man - Adam (the first man, and therefore symbolical of all men) walked naked in the Garden of Eden, from which he was expelled for disobedience of God's law. His expulsion from Eden was followed soon afterwards by his wearing of clothes. Thus sin and the concealment of nakedness are notions which are traditionally associated.

The Household Steward - it is to be noted that by wearing the garb of a steward the Common Man becomes a character inside the play.

The Century of the Common Man - the implication of this remark is that History is not merely the record of great men or of important events, since in every age the Common Man is largely and intimately concerned with what goes on about him.

ACT I • SCENE 1

Sir Thomas More - at this stage of the play, More is a man of great eminence, an intimate associate of King Henry VIII.

Rich - Sir Richard Rich (1496—1567)
(See Character Sketches)

Every man has his price - this cynical judgement is usually attributed to the statesman Walpole (1676-1745) yet is most appropriate to the notions of Machiavelli (1469-1527). It means that one may persuade a man to do anything (e.g. betray his principles or his friends) if he be offered a sufficient reward.

Bricks-and-mortar - houses; buildings in general.

Buy a man with suffering - Momentarily, More thinks that Rich is supporting the notion that some men may actually be tempted by the prospect of suffering or even of martyrdom.

You should go back to Cambridge - While at Cambridge, Rich had shown great academic promise. More believed that he should not become involved in affairs of state, so that he wouldn't fall to temptation.

The Cardinal's outer doorman - Cardinal Wolsey, when Lord Chancellor, was reputed to be the richest man in England, and one of the most powerful in Europe. Lines of important people waited on him daily to ask his favours. Rich had hoped to rise by Wolsey's influence, but so far he had not even been allowed to get beyond the outer doorman, whom he would need to bribe handsomely. These lines demonstrate Wolsey's great power and wealth, and the difficulty of gaining an audience of him with a view to attracting his favourable attention.

Duke of Norfolk - Thomas Howard, Earl of Surrey and Duke of Norfolk (1473—1554).

Office - paid position with the government, often a sinecure.

The Dean of St. Paul's - John Colet (1467—1519) became the Dean of St. Paul's Cathedral in 1501. Colet re-established St. Paul's School (still one of the well-known English "public" schools). The "New Learning", with which More, Colet and Erasmus were associated in England, sought to promote a purified form of Christianity, illuminated by classical philosophy. For this reason they were concerned to stimulate the study of Greek and Latin, which subjects were part of the curriculum of this new school.

The new school - Colet actually re-established St. Paul's School between 1508 and 1512, with wealth inherited from his father.

The Court of Requests - this special Court of Law was established by Cardinal Wolsey and came to be known as the "Court of Poor Men's Causes", since it dealt largely with the grievances of the common people. Catherine Anger had once made More a present hoping that when she later brought her case before him he would pronounce judgement in her favour. Thomas Cromwell afterwards tried (Act II) to use this incident to discredit More.

In office they offer you all sorts of things - in earlier days, men in public offices were commonly offered bribes. More apparently considers that Rich may easily give in to bribery, and that he will be less open to temptation should he become a teacher, remote from the world of affairs.

A coat of arms - the offer of the manor house and the village perhaps included a coat of arms or heraldic device of the family which had originally occupied the estate.

I shouldn't be surprised - these words are apparently intended to demonstrate More's vagueness and unconcern for material possessions.

I was commanded into office - More's career was in marked contrast to that of Rich, since he achieved favour without seeking it. (See Character Sketches).

Alice - Lady Alice, More's second wife.

Meg - diminutive form of Margaret. Lady Margaret was More's favourite daughter, who eventually married William Roper. (See Character Sketches)

No falcon could stoop - in hawking or falconry the bird was trained to pounce or swoop on its prey after first hovering high in the air above it. "Stoop" is a variant of "Swoop".

Don't care - "don't" instead of "doesn't" was once considered correct usage.

Cast - in hunting or hawking, a search for the scent or tracks of game birds and animals.

Aristotle - Greek philosopher (383—322 B.C.) whose many philosophical treatises formed the basis of science in the Middle Ages. Rich is evidently trying to display his learning.

Exhalation - that which is breathed out or exhaled; the act of breathing out.

Act of God - violent force or manifestation of nature, such as an earthquake or hurricane, which is beyond the control of man.

God's body - to swear by God's body or parts thereof was quite commonplace at this period. However, it seems somewhat uncouth in the mouth of a woman, and may be intended to reflect her lower origin.

City wife - Lady More is asserting that she is not a City merchant's wife, who might be ignorant of courtly and aristocratic pastimes. Actually, she came from the class that she seems to despise.

Master Rich is newly converted to the doctrines of Machiavelli - More suggests teasingly that Rich has forsaken classical philosophy for the new ideas expressed in Machiavelli's "The Prince". In Norfolk's presence, Rich would prefer to enjoy a reputation for conservatism. Later, when talking with Cromwell, he endeavours to appear progressive in his views. In opposition to More, Rich is a man of scant principle - an opportunist.

The Cardinal's Secretary - Cromwell was appointed secretary to Cardinal

Wolsey, the Lord Chancellor, in 1525.

Howard - this was the Norfolk's family name. More addresses him familiarly, since they are close friends.

A farrier's son - Cromwell's father was a blacksmith, while Wolsey's father was a butcher or grazier. Aristocrats such as the Duke of Norfolk tended to resent being subordinates of such "upstarts".

Talk of the Cardinal's Secretary - according to an old adage, if you speak of the Devil you will be sure to see his tail. More adapts this saying on receiving a letter from Cromwell, who had recently been appointed to this position.

The King's business .... the Queen's business - the question of the King's divorce from Catherine of Aragon.

Is there a boat? - More had evidently been summoned by Wolsey to his Chancellory at Hampton Court Palace. At this period, travellers in London commonly used the River Thames as an alternative to the dirty and dangerous streets. More lived at Chelsea, then a mere village some distance from London. His garden reached down to the Thames - a safe and convenient means of travel for him. Up river was Hampton Court Palace, near Richmond, down river was Westminster Palace, while further down still was the infamous Tower of London.

Richmond - a town in Surrey, about nine or ten miles up river from the capital.

New Inn - one of the Inns of Court, where law students read with a view to being called to the bar. (i.e. become barristers).

Hounslow - an area of Middlesex, now a suburb of London. In the fifteenth century it was a wild expanse of country suitable only for hawking and hunting.

The ground's hard at Hounslow, Alice - apparently while riding there, Cardinal Wolsey had once fallen off his horse.

Some day someone's going to ask him for something that he wants to keep - these comments appear to be in the nature of a dire prediction so far as More is concerned.

ACT I • SCENE 2

Wolsey - Thomas Cardinal Wolsey (1475-1530) (See Character Sketches)

The Latin dispatch - all official letters at this period were written in Latin, such being the lingua franca of diplomacy. This particular dispatch was a letter to the Pope asking him to declare the invalidity of Henry's marriage to Catherine of Aragon, or to appoint a commission with the authority to determine the issue.

A little common sense - it is noteworthy that both Cardinal Wolsey and the Common Man, in his role as Steward, use the same expression.

The Council - the King's Council.

He's been to play in the muck again - a contemptuous way of suggesting that the King has been visiting Anne Boleyn.

Change of dynasty - The House of Tudor was established by Henry VII after his defeat of Richard III at the Battle of Bosworth Field in 1485. Henry's subsequent marriage united the rival Houses of York and Lancaster. On his death in 1509 his second surviving son assumed the throne as Henry VIII.

Catherine's his wife - the reference is to Catherine of Aragon (1485—1536), daughter of Ferdinand and Isabella of Spain.

A dispensation - an official exemption from the provisions of a Law of the Roman Catholic Church.

The Pope - Clement VII, who was Pope from 1523 to 1534.

The Yorkist Wars: - the Wars of the Roses (1455—85) between the Houses of York and Lancaster. These disastrous civil wars were brought to an end when the Lancastrian Henry Tudor defeated the Yorkist King Richard III in 1485 and came to the throne as Henry VII. Wolsey asserts that peace depends on the continuance of the Tudor dynasty being assured by a male heir.

Certain measures - the Cardinal is apparently hinting that the Pope's decision may be influenced by the threat of reforming the Church in England.

He relights the candle - this act is evidently one of symbolism on More's part.

Who will deal with all this paper, after me? You? Fisher? Suffolk? - The Cardinal poses the question of his successor to the Lord Chancellorship. Fisher was the Bishop of Rochester, while the Duke of Suffolk was the King's brother-in-law, and an influential member of the Council. It happened that Fisher was to be executed shortly before More, and in the same circumstances. More succeeded Wolsey as Lord Chancellor, Norfolk became President of the Council, and Suffolk the Vice-President.

You should have been a cleric - Wolsey suggests that More ought to have been a priest because he is not worldly enough for affairs of state. More's reply is shrewd, since he is aware that Wolsey is a very worldly churchman.

ACT I • SCENE 3

Chapuys - Eustace Chapuys, the Ambassador of Charles V, King of Spain, and Holy Roman Emperor. (See Character Sketches)

Charles - Charles V, King of Spain (1519—56) and Holy Roman Emperor (1519—56), was the nephew of Queen Catherine of Aragon, the first wife of Henry VIII.

A nod is as good as a wink to a blind horse - this old adage means: "There is no need to tell me in more specific terms."

Dominus Vobiscum - "The Lord be with you."

Spirituo tuo - More makes the customary response in Latin - "and with thy spirit".

The river looks very black tonight - the double significance of this remark is worthy of note.

ACT I • SCENE 4

Master Roper - William Roper (1496—1578) (See Character Sketches)

Called to the Bar - admitted to the profession of barrister. A barrister is a legal advocate who is qualified to plead on behalf of a client in a Court of Law.

The City - the commercial and financial centre of London, an area consisting today of roughly one square mile, situated in the East End.

Heretic - one who denies the authority of the Roman Catholic Church. Roper was for a time a convinced Protestant.

Doctor Luther - Martin Luther (1483—1546), German monk and priest, and the mainspring of the German Reformation.

Luther's an excommunicate - Martin Luther had been excommunicated from the Roman Catholic Church in 1521.

It's a shop - Luther's revolt against the Roman Catholic Church began with his attack on the sale of indulgences, that is, the practice of pardoning sins in return for money payments, or the promise thereof.

Joblots - job lots - a term used to describe casual sales in large quantities. Roper also suggests that the Church annulled or cancelled marriages in return for money payments.

Inns of Court - where barristers and would-be barristers congregated in large numbers.

Antichrist - the Devil; Christ's legendary opponent, supposedly capable of assuming a variety of guises, with the object of undermining Christianity.

Oh, one more or less - it is noteworthy that, by this remark, More ends a serious discussion with a characteristic sense of humour.

Levelling talk - More jestingly chides Lady Alice for talking as though all men were equal - a revolutionary idea in the 15th century.

The Tower - the Tower of London was the ancient fortress where rebels and traitors of rank were imprisoned and executed. More's teasing remark contains a grim reminder of the dangers always awaiting the statesman who erred or fell from favour.

Roughly piles them into his basket - when the Common Man puts the Cardinal's robe and hat into his property basket, he is indicating to the audience wordlessly that Wolsey has fallen from power, a point which he proceeds to elaborate.

Whether we follow tradition - it is to be noted that the role of the Common Man is now external to the play for the time being, and that the events he speaks of occupy a period of some three to four years.

Leicester - the city and county town of Leicestershire. Cardinal Wolsey died there and was buried in the Lady Chapel of St. Mary's Abbey.

Under charge of High Treason - in 1529, as the result of the concerted action of his several enemies, Cardinal Wolsey was removed from the Lord Chancellorship and banished to York. Subsequently he was charged with High Treason, on the grounds that he had taken an active part in the King's excommunication.

By his writings - More's best known literary works are his *History of Richard III* and his *Utopia*.

ACT I • SCENE 5

Hampton Court - a palace (still standing) on the Thames above Richmond. It was built by Wolsey for himself but eleven years later, in 1526 , was presented by him to the king.

The Great Harry - The early fifteenth century was a period of intense naval rivalry between England, Spain and France. The size and armament of ships were matters of great concern. The so-called *Great Harry* (actually the *Henri Grace a Dieu*) was the ship that had taken Henry on his famous visit to King Francis in 1520. The reference is therefore an anachronism.

Deptford - an outer suburb of London, approximately three miles southeast of the City. In the 16th Century, it was the site of a large and important naval dockyard.

Sir Thomas is a man - suggesting that he is capable of changing his mind, or submitting to pressure.

Dominican - member of the Dominican Order of the friars founded by St. Dominic in 1215.

Soapy - colloquial term meaning: ingratiating; oily; oleaginous; smooth.

No man can serve two masters - see St. Matthew 6:24.

A fanfare of trumpets; plainsong - the fanfare suggests King and State, while the term plainsong, a non-metrical melody used in religious services, is clearly indicative of the Church. Thus the playwright contrives to symbolise the two contentious elements of the play, and anticipates the conflict of the ensuing scene.

ACT I • SCENE 6

Vespers - an evening church service; the second last of the seven periods of each day, set aside by the Roman Catholic Church for prayer, worship and meditation.

Cassock - long black cloak, buttoned down the front, such as is commonly affected by priests.

Cleric - priest; member of the Clergy.

Hose - long stockings of the type commonly worn in the 16th century.

Henry - King Henry VIII (1491—1547)

There is no end to the making of books - see Ecclesiastes 12:12.

Your Grace's Book - King Henry's defence of the Pope's authority against the heresies of Lutheranism was known as *Assertio Septem Sacramentorum (Assertion of the Seven Sacraments)*. The seven sacraments of the Church are baptism, holy communion, confirmation, confession, ordination, matrimony and extreme unction. The significance, validity and importance of some of these were disputed by Luther. The King's support of the Pope was rewarded by his being granted the title of *Fidei Defensor (Defender of the Faith)*, a designation which, ironically, he and successive monarchs retained even after the breach with Rome.

The Bishop of Rome - one of the Pope's titles. The King appears to consider that the Pontiff's authority should be restricted to the See of Rome.

It was never merry in England while we had cardinals amongst us - this remark is commonly credited to the Duke of Norfolk or the Duke of Suffolk, and was made at a meeting of the King's Council when it seemed evident that Cardinals Wolsey and Campeggio were hedging in the matter of the royal divorce. Wolsey, impatient and resentful of criticism, is said to have reacted angrily.

Doggett's Bank - an imaginary physical feature of the Thames Estuary.

Tilbury - a town in the estuary of the River Thames; it still has an extensive area of docks, wharves and the like.

Roads - roads in this sense are sites adjacent to the shoreline where ships are able to anchor or "tie up".

Wick - the fabric at the centre of a candle or oil lamp where the flame burns. Here it is used metaphorically.

The Great Seal - the emblem of the office of the Lord Chancellor. A seal is an engraved stamp by which an impression is made in sealing-wax attached to a document, thereby signifying official sanction.

I stand in peril of my soul - the King either believed or affected to believe that he had sinned against the law of God by marrying Catherine of Aragon, his brother's widow. In the matter of the Law of Consanguinity, there is an apparent conflict between Deuteronomy and Leviticus.

The Holy See - the seat of the power or authority of the Bishop of Rome (the Pope); hence the rank, office, power, etc., of the Pope.

Son after son she's borne me - Queen Catherine had given birth to four sons, none of whom had survived for more than a few weeks.

I have a daughter - Mary, born 1516, was eventually to become Queen (1553—58).

It is my bounden duty - the King is concerned to establish the Tudor succession upon a male heir.

St. Peter - The Apostle Peter, regarded as the first Pope, and the founder of the Christian Church.

Princes of the Church - the prelates of the period vied with the secular rulers in their power, wealth and splendor. The King is using the expression satirically, since he apparently believes that the Church has established a rival sovereignty within the land, which was harmful to his authority.

The Bishop of Rome with the Emperor's knife to his throat - Spanish and German troops of Charles V, the nephew of Catherine of Aragon, had laid waste to Rome in 1527, and had taken Pope Clement VII prisoner. It may be presumed that, even after his release, the Pontiff was still subject to some degree of pressure, and was not entirely free to express his own opinion.

Mouths me - quotes to me (perhaps ad nauseum).

Deuteronomy - this probably refers to Chapter 17, in which is stated that issues in dispute must be referred to the priests, whose decision is to be regarded as final.

nice - scrupulous; fastidious; particular as to detail.

Woman, mind your house - an apparently harmless remark; however, it appears ironical, when one bears in mind the response of Lady Alice.

Lady Anne - Anne Boleyn (1507—36). A member of a noble family, she spent much of her early life in France. While her association with the King probably began as early as 1523, her name was not openly linked with his until some four years later. In September, 1533, she gave birth to a daughter, Elizabeth, who was destined to become Queen. Accused of adultery and other offences in 1536, she was executed in the same year.

A sacrament of the Church - More here refers to the sacrament of marriage.

Soupcon - suggestion; trifle; suspicion; small quantity or amount.

Joshua's trumpet - according to the bible story, the walls of Jericho fell down at the noise of trumpets sounded by the priests, whereupon Joshua proceeded to capture the city. More suggests that his daughter's resistance appears to collapse, when her lover speaks of his conscience.

I've been offered a seat in the next Parliament - Roper actually became a Member of Parliament for Bamber, Sussex, in 1529.

The money-changers in the temple - see St. Matthew 21:12 and St. John 2:13—16.

Sophistication - subtle or clever arguments that are calculated to deceive. The Sophists of ancient Greece were teachers of philosophy who cultivated skill in reasoning and debate, but were eventually accused of degenerating into quibblers.

Jumped the gun - a runner "jumps the gun" when he starts his race before the signal shot has been fired. Rich's feelings of guilt make him sensitive to atmosphere, so that he unconsciously reacts to hostility which has not even been expressed.

This is the golden calf - a false god or idol. See Exodus 32.

Moloch - Phoenician and Ammonite god to which human beings were frequently cruelly and wantonly sacrificed.

Put about - changed direction, a metaphor derived from sailing. It expresses a contrast with the "firm ground" of More's convictions.

Burgundy - any wine, whether red or white, made in Burgundy, a former province of France.

ACT I • SCENE 7

Collector of Revenues for York - York was and continues to be the most important See in England, after that of Canterbury. Thus, while the Archbishop of Canterbury is the Primate of all-England, the Archbishop of York is the Primate of England.

High Constable - at this period the High Constable was the senior official of the Royal household.

Sir Thomas Paget - this may be presumed to be a fictitious name.

May I say "friendship"? - it is to be noted that Rich used the same words, when speaking to More in the introductory act of the play.

The embankment - the built-up banks of the River Thames.

Litigant - a person engaged in a law-suit or legal action.

Chancery - at this period the highest court of law (except Parliament), which was presided over by the Lord Chancellor. It was largely concerned with matters of conflicting interests between litigants.

ACT II • SCENE 1

The Church of England - in 1531, the King was declared by Parliament to be the "Protector and Only Supreme Head of the Church and Clergy in England".

You wouldn't last six months in Spain - the Inquisition had been reorganized in Spain in 1478 with the object of eliminating all traces of heresy. The methods of the Inquisition were entirely ruthless, and often took the form of torture and execution by burning.

The bishops in Convocation - in fact, the bishops had acknowledged King Henry as the Supreme Head of the Church of England in February, 1531. However, there remained widespread opposition among the clergy. Accordingly, in 1532, Warham, Archbishop of Canterbury, suggested a compromise by the addition of the words "so far as the laws of Christ permit". At Canterbury, Convocation accepted this without protest, while the Convocation of York submitted six weeks later. More regarded the so-called "Submission of the Clergy" as a betrayal of the principles of the Church.

Canterbury - city and county town of Kent, the site of the oldest cathedral in England, around which congregated the members of the first Christian mission to that country, despatched by Pope Gregory the Great in 597.

The Archbishop - William Warham, Archbishop of Canterbury from 1503—1532, the immediate predecessor of the better known Thomas Cranmer.

The Act of Supremacy - this Act, by which Henry became Supreme Head of all the Church in England (Anglicana Ecclesia), became law in 1534.

You've a wife now - Roper had married Lady Margaret. More was cautious, believing that one should be careful not to involve one's family in the risks attendant upon unpopular political and religious beliefs.

A faint radiance - a halo, or aura of light, with which painters commonly circumscribe the heads of the devout and holy. More is being facetious.

Socrates - the Greek philosopher (470—399 B.C.), noted for his idealism and clarity of thought in ethical and political matters. Accused of corrupting the young, Socrates was sentenced to death, a fate which he might easily have escaped, had he recanted.

Erasmus - Desiderius Erasmus (1466?—1536), was the great Dutch scholar, a leading figure of the New Learning and a close personal friend of More.

I've no taste for hemlock - More means that he has no wish to become a martyr in the manner of Socrates, who was permitted to take his own life by drinking hemlock.

Dominus vobiscum filii mei! - The Lord be with you, my children.

Et cum spirituo tuo, excellensis! - And with thy spirit, excellency.

Things are very different, there, my lord. There they are ready - Chapuys is referring to the discontent in the northern counties occasioned by the plundering of the monasteries. This eventually gave rise in 1536 to the Pilgrimage of Grace.

This isn't 'Reformation'; this is war against the Church! - in common with other humanists like Colet and Erasmus, More advocated the internal reform of the Church, rather than overt rebellion.

Vicar of God - God's substitute or representative.

The King accepts your resignation - More's resignation from the Lord Chancellorship was accepted in May, 1532.

He will be your good lord - one of the King's promises destined to be dishonoured.

The Border - the troubled and often hostile border region between England and Scotland.

The Old Alliance - that between Scotland and France. Should trouble occur on the Scottish border, it would be necessary to watch France, for fear that she intervene on behalf of her ancient ally.

Dago - a term of contempt for a Latin - a sneering allusion to the Spanish Ambassador, Chapuys.

Sit by the fire and make goslings in the ash - Nicholas Harpsfield, in his *Life of More*, quotes Lady Alice as asking, "Will you sit still by the fire, and make goslings in the ashes with a stick as children do?"

You'd dance him to the block, like David with a harp - Lady Alice appears to mean that Roper would gladly see More in the role of a martyr displaying his religious zeal. (See Samuel 2:6)

The marriage he'll then make - in fact the King secretly married Anne Boleyn on January 25, 1533, and on June 1 of the same year she was proclaimed Queen.

Even stevens - Cockney rhyming slang, meaning equally or evenly balanced.

ACT II • SCENE 2

Cato - Cato the Elder (234—149 B.C.), a Roman consul, famous for his honesty in the conduct of public affairs.

Lincoln - city and county town of Lincolnshire, an eastern county situated between the Rivers Wash and Humber.

In April 1526 - it should be noted that this date sets the time at which the play opens.

A horse that won't run - plan or scheme that will not succeed. Cromwell, in his reply, continues the metaphor.

ACT II • SCENE 3

I have a Royal Commission - from King Charles of Spain, the Holy Roman Emperor.

I have a personal letter for you - More's political caution is clearly demonstrated by his refusal to accept this.

A huge bundle of bracken - according to Nicholas Harpsfield in his *Life of More* he "was enforced and compelled for lack of other fuel, every night before he went to bed, to cause a great bundle of fern to be brought into his own chamber and with the blaze whereof to warm himself, his wife and his children, and so without any other fires to go into their beds".

The money from the Bishops - realizing his needs, More was offered four thousand pounds by the Clergy in Convocation. It was supposedly offered him as a reward for his many writings in defence of the Church, but More feared that his acceptance of it would be misconstrued to his disadvantage.

There's a gentleman here from Hampton Court - this announcement advances the action of the play to February, 1534, when More, in fact, appeared before the Commissioners for interrogation.

Witty...wit - this is a play on the different meanings of wit.

Pragmatist - in this context, the word refers to a man who judges purely by results, rather than principles; one who is expedient; a competent lawyer, as distinct from a scholarly jurist.

ACT II • SCENE 4

That's a nice gown you have Richard - the irony of this remark is worthy of note.

If you could bring yourself to agree with the Universities, the Bishops and the Parliament - Cromwell, is drawing More's attention to the fact of his isolated position. Almost alone of the leading men of his day, More refused to give approval of the King's divorce and subsequent re-marriage. To such a man as Cromwell, his attitude would appear to be one of foolish arrogance.

Holy Maid of Kent - the nun, Elizabeth Barton (1506—1534) was apparently a victim of religious mania, which manifested itself in frequent trances and hysterical fits. Maintaining that she was in direct communication with the Blessed Virgin, she prophesied evil for the king, and condemned his divorce. Eventually she was tried for treason, forced to recant and was executed. More said, at the time she was charged, that her predictions were merely "such as any simple woman might speak out of her own wit". At this stage of the play. More is being accused of meeting her, of corresponding with her, and of not divulging all that he knew of her.

Canon law - ecclesiastical law; church law.

These are terrors for children - in February, 1534, a Bill of Attainder against Fisher and More was introduced into the House of Lords. More successfully answered the charges which Cromwell preferred against him before the Commissioners. The actual words he used were: "My Lords, these terrors be arguments for children, not for me".

ACT II • SCENE 5

Between the upper and nether millstones - in a position to be crushed or squeezed.

You have a son - the point of this veiled threat is that if Norfolk should quarrel with the King he might be accused of high treason, in which case, if found guilty, his son would be legally deprived of his inheritance.

We're supposed to be the arrogant ones - Norfolk refers to the alleged arrogance of the aristocracy to which he belongs.

The Sermon on the Mount - see St. Matthew 5:7.

You'll labour like Thomas Aquinas over a rat-dog's pedigree - More means that the aristocracy are indifferent to Christian principles, but are profoundly interested in the breeding of sporting dogs.

Thomas Aquinas - St Thomas Aquinas (1225-1274), an outstanding philosopher of the Roman Catholic Church, famous for his mastery of religious doctrine and his polemical skill.

Somewhere back along your pedigree - More is amplifying his earlier remark concerning the spaniel. According to him, Norfolk is a traitor to his own soul, in the same way that the animal was false to its own nature.

There's to be a new Act - a reference to the Act of Succession (March, 1534), which, in fact, preceded the Act of Supremacy (November, 1534). The sequence is changed for dramatic reasons.

Iron grills now descend - it is to be noted that the Tower, a notorious place of imprisonment, is indicated by a simple contrivance.

Nearer the knuckle - less likely to be acceptable: less attractive to the squeamish.

An envelope descends swiftly before him - the Common Man's comments on the ultimate fate of the members of the Commission provide a good example of the "Alienation Effect" associated with Brecht.

ACT II • SCENE 6

Act of Succession - by the terms of this act any offspring of Anne Boleyn would be regarded as the king's heirs.

Material - the word is here used in its legal sense, meaning germane or relevant.

Some men think the Earth is round - the theory of the Polish astronomer, Copernicus (1473—1543), was still in dispute.

I defy anyone to live in that cell for a year - More had originally been committed to the Tower in April, 1534, and was a sick man.

The Lieutenant - the title of the governor of the Tower of London.

Cross of vestment - the cross embroidered or woven on his stole.

ACT II • SCENE 7

If we lived in a State where virtue was profitable - More appears to be musing upon his own *Utopia*.

Well, has Eve run out of apples? - More is asking if his daughter has ceased to tempt him. Margaret has tried desperately to convince him to take the oath, but she is now silent.

The rack - an instrument of torture. Margaret is tormenting her father by telling him how badly they are doing at home.

The worst that they may do to me - More feared that he might be hanged, drawn and quartered. By comparison, execution by beheading was merciful.

Upper gallery - Bishop Fisher was confined in a cell above.

ACT II • SCENE 8

The Hall of Westminster - part of the old Royal Palace, built by William II in 1097. It was the scene of many famous trials. More was brought here in July, 1535.

Forthink - think over again; reconsider; express regret; recant.

My lords, I thank you ...... - what More is made to say in the play forms an interesting example of literary compression. According to R.W. Chambers, in his *Thomas More*, the accused man's words were actually as follows: "My Lords, I humbly thank you for your great good will. Howbeit, I make my petition unto Almighty God that it may please Him to maintain me in this my honest mind, to the last hour that I shall live. And concerning the matters you charge me withal, the articles are so prolix and long that I fear, what for my long imprisonment, what for my disease and present weakness, that neither my wit, nor memory, nor voice will serve to make sufficient answer.

Bishop Fisher was executed this morning - in fact, the Bishop was beheaded on June 22, to be followed by More, on July 6.

Death....comes for us all - part of More's *Dialogue of Comfort against Tribulations*, written during his imprisonment in the Tower of London, reads as follows: "Knew you not that Christ must suffer passion, and by that way enter into his kingdom? Who can for very shame desire to enter into the Kingdom of Christ with ease, when himself entered not into his own without pain?"

The Kingdom - The Kingdom of God.

Betoken - mean; signify;

Qui tacet consentire - "He who keeps silent appears to consent." More was very careful not to speak in opposition to the King's claims. Maintaining silence cannot be legally construed as opposition; in law it is understood to indicate unspoken consent.

Sir Richard Southwell and Master Palmer - in fact both these men attended the trial, and each of them contradicted Rich's testimony.

The Red dragon - the traditional national emblem of Wales.

For Wales?......But for Wales! - evidently More does not entertain a very high opinion of Wales. His remarks demonstrate his sense of humour, especially when one considers the circumstances in which they are uttered.

Magna Carta - this document, signed and sealed in 1215 by King John is generally regarded as the basis of the rights and liberties of the English. It contains an affirmation of the rights and privileges of the Church.

Coronation Oath - a British sovereign to this day undertakes as part of the Coronation Oath, to support the Church "as by law established."

Now we plainly see that you are malicious- by the Act of Treasons of 1534, it became high treason, after February 1, 1535, in speech or in writing "maliciously to deny" to the King his personal dignities, titles or prerogatives. It is to this that Cromwell apparently refers. Historically, the statement is credited to the Duke of Norfolk, but the dramatic purpose of putting it into the mouth of Cromwell is quite obvious.

ACT II • SCENE 9

My master had easel and gall - according to the bible, Christ on the Cross was given easel and gall to drink. Easel was vinegar, while gall was probably a vegetable poison. There is, however, a tradition that the two were mixed to produce an opiate. (Matthew 27:48).

Character Sketches

Sir Thomas More

The outstanding character in the play is, of course, Sir Thomas More himself. The dramatist has seen him as a man in his late forties, although in fact the play will not stand up to exact chronological tests. The action starts at a point when the end is inevitable. In the very first scene—that is to say what would be called the "exposition" scene of a well-made play—the audience is introduced to young Rich, who later in the play will turn out to be a double-dyed traitor to More, and the incident of the goblet, a gift from one of More's litigants, will be introduced.

More is essentially a social man with a real sense of the importance of family life. Bolt has himself referred to More's "splendid social adjustment". More was not a rebel, one of civilisation's discontents: on the other hand he was almost a complete conformist. Bolt has likened him to the hero of Albert Camus's *La Chute*—a man "almost indecently successful".

The play is entirely concerned with the reversal in More's fortunes. We are not shown the steps by which More ascended to his leading position in the state. When the curtain rises he is already a renowned figure, and Rich appears as a young man "on the make" who has singled out More precisely because he was a leading counsellor of the King, a man who seemed to have "the golden touch"—a man who effortlessly had "made the grade".

Yet nowhere is More made to appear conscious of his own rank. He is far more concerned with his family; as he says,

> I was commanded into office. It was inflicted on me—Can't you believe that?

There is no sense of self-importance; yet the part of More is not an exercise in self-humiliation. He is essentially the soul of the play—but he scorns heroics of popularised biography. He is far removed from the operatic type of character as possible. He does not set out to be a martyr; the author is at some pains to reveal his weaknesses rather than his symbolical strength. He is pictured as pale, middle-sized with spindly legs, not robust. He has no stereotyped façade to present to the public. He knows the world, but he never sets himself up as a "smart knocker". Cynicism is not his stock in trade. Although his mind was cast in a witty mould he had not the Falstaffian gift of making himself a butt of others' wit.

Early in the play he advises Rich on the value of a quiet life, but that ambitious self-seeker can only think that More is joking, when in fact he was never more serious. Many are the aspects of More that are not stressed: his great scholarship and his religious ascetism are only touched on in the lightest of terms. One would never realise, for example, that this More was the author of one of the legendary books of all times— the *Utopia*.

He is pictured as devout, in an age when religion was taken very seriously. Yet a careful observer of people, such as Wolsey, from the first realised that it is precisely this "moral squint" which distinguishes More from a thousand other lawyers and self-seekers. It is Wolsey who says, "With just a little common sense you could have been a statesman".

More is shown in contact with many different characters—with Cromwell, with Rich, with Henry, with Norfolk, with Chapuys—but always we feel that he is an individual character. Bolt had himself stated in his Preface:

> He was respectably not nobly born, in...the progressive class of the epoch...A visitors' book at his house in Chelsea would have looked like a Sixteenth Century *Who's Who*: Holbein, Erasmus,

> Colet, everybody. He corresponded with the greatest minds in Europe as the representative and acknowledged champion of the New Learning in England...He adored and was adored by his own large family. He parted with more than most men when he parted with his life, for he accepted and enjoyed his social context.

Above all he reposed a great trust in the workings of the Law—and in this respect he was a traditional Englishman. He felt that he could rely on the Law:

> More's trust in the law was his trust in his society; his desperate sheltering beneath the forms of the law was his determination to remain within the shelter of society. Cromwell's contemptuous shattering of the forms of law by an unconcealed act of perjury showed how fragile for any individual is that shelter. Legal or illegal had no further meaning.

More is not depicted as a religious zealot; in this respect Bolt has minimised the evidence. A characteristic which has impressed many students of More, his zeal against heretics, is here confined to a stern treatment of his son-in-law William Roper, who at the beginning of the play is a passionate Lutheran but shifts his position as the play develops.

The play revolves around two poles of action—the events that led up to the martyrdom, and the family circle. It is in keeping with what the historians have told us, that he was a plain man, completely without that exhibitionism and egotism which is too often the hall mark of the "self-made" man. In an age that was notorious for its costly dress, his own clothing was modest, the only sign of his status being a gold chain said to be a Lancastrian badge instituted by Henry IV and symbolic of his office as Chancellor of the Duchy of Lancaster. We have it on the authority of Erasmus that he wore no other ornaments, no silks, no velvets. The one genuine portrait of More painted by a contemporary was owned by Henry VIII and thrown out of the window by Anne Boleyn.

His family circle was his real life, including his house and his garden. In the play this family circle is represented by his daughter Margaret and his wife Alice. Even in his own family circle there were seemingly those who wondered why More made such a fuss of the oath-taking. Alice, his wife, thought so; she would have agreed with Henry Pattesen, the court-jester, who wondered why Sir Thomas More would not bring himself to swear the oath, since the court-jester had found no difficulty! Alice puts her finger on the real issue when she says in response to More's direct question, "What would you *want* me to do?"—"Be ruled!." /If you won't rule him [Henry VIII], be ruled."/ To which More replies, "There's a little...little area where I must rule myself". He would not surrender his conscience. Alice beseeches him to reconsider—to stay friends with the King, and More replies, "Whatever can be done by smiling , you may rely on me to do."

His family circle never seemed to have understood the man. Neither

Roper, who regards him as too sophisticated, nor Alice who regards him as too head-strong, has the faintest conception of the real More. Roper sees in More a man who is sophisticated. To which More replies that it is not sophistication, but sheer simplicity. "The law...I know what's legal not what's right. And I'll stick to what's legal". Roper maintains that as a result More would give the Devil himself the benefit of the law, in contrast to himself, who would cut down every law in England to get at the Devil. To the argument that man must give the Devil the benefit of the law, if only for the safety which the law will provide, Roper says that he had long suspected it. "This is the golden calf; the law's your god."

But More is unshaken: "Whoever hunts for me...will find me hiding in the thickets of the law! And I'll hide my daughter with me!" Summing up his position More tries to reassure his family, "I have not disobeyed my sovereign. I truly believe no man in England is safer than myself." When Alice asks, "Why then does Cromwell collect information about you?" he retorts, "I'm a prominent figure. Someone somewhere's collecting information about Cromwell". Such is the position at the fall of the curtain in Act I. In Act II, the time has come when More is forced to abandon all reliance on legalism and to rely on first principles.

In the second act, the threads of the action laid down in the first act are drawn tightly—escape is impossible. Nothing short of a *deus ex machina* will enable More to extricate himself, and the dramatist no less than the historian scorns such a superficial device. Rich and Cromwell are shown trying to incriminate More through the shabby device of the charge of embezzlement—the case of Catherine Anger in the Court of Requests. This, as indeed was inevitable, breaks down like a pack of cards. But the enemies of More are inflexible. As Cromwell grimly says, "The King is not pleased with you". He puts the matter even more plainly to his underling Rich when he says,

> The King wants Sir Thomas More either to bless his marriage or to be destroyed. Either will do.

And since More has a conscience and will not either explicitly or implicitly "bless" the marriage, then his destruction is a foregone conclusion. Every step in the sequence of events is as inevitable as if it had been planned with inescapable logic. We find More in the Tower and over him the rack hangs menacingly. Even the walls drip—it is hard to say whether from the river or from the blood of those who have paid for their "treason" with their lives.

In a last moving scene Margaret and Alice try to persuade him. Margaret cries, "Haven't you done as much as God can reasonably want?", and Alice tries to jerk him into a sense of proportion when she declares, "Are you content to be shut up here with mice and rats when you might have been at home with us?"

From that moment the descent into cruel tragedy is swift. There follows the trial, the perjury of Rich and the sentence. The last we see of More is when he turns to the Headsman and bids him not to be afraid of his office. "You send me to God."

More's wife and daughter are the only two named women in the play, and in the setting of a historical play of the sixteenth century their parts are necessarily small. Their presence gives variety in characterisation and also throws More's integrity into greater relief. He is seen to plough a lone furrow at home as well as in the state. His wife and his favourite daughter (the representatives in the play of his family) plead with him to reconsider—and in vain. At home and in the world outside all are against him, and this throws More's honesty and bravery into greater prominence.

The Common Man

The character of the Common Man has given rise to much critcal discussion. One of the causes of the sudden popularity of historical plays during the 'sixties is undoubtedly the growing influence of Bertolt Brecht, the German director, poet and dramatist, whose influence has dominated the contemporary theatre of our age. Between 1937 and 1945 Brecht, a fugitive from Nazi Germany, wrote a series of plays, many of which are now recognized as masterpieces in their own right. Perhaps the greatest of these was the historical play *Galileo*. Brecht's influence has been felt in the European and American theatre in two ways. In the first place all his work has a humanist and political awareness, and even at times a teacher-like note running through it. Brecht has frequently appeared as a theorist of the theatre, and it is probably not too much to say that his writings on the theatre have exerted as much influence as those of Stanislavsky.

But he was not merely a theorist. He was a practical man of the theatre and it was because of this that he was recognised as one of the greatest figures in the contemporary theatre. Particularly important has been his concept of the Alienation Effect. In brief, the idea behind this is that Brecht envisages the theatre, not as a place for the satisfaction of wish-fulfilment, but as a highly *critical* place, and he requires of actors and audience alike a critical detachment from the play and its performance. Brecht's theory first and foremost requires the dramatist and the actor to use a deliberate technique to keep the audience in a state of critical awareness. They must be constantly aware that they are acting in a *play*; they must never forget that they are actors, they must never identify themselves with the characters they are portraying.

Actually this theory, although modern, had been presented as long ago as the time of Diderot, who had suggested very much the same idea in his *Paradox sur Comedien*, that the actor must never "lose himself" in the role he is creating, but must always stand out, a critical spectator, uncommitted and uninvolved. The playwright is an artistic fabricator, and the theatre is not to be confused with narrow realism or naturalism. To take an instance from the production of Shakespeare. The English actor Beerbohm Tree produced *A Midsummer Night's Dream* in such an authentic and "real" fashion that his stage was cluttered up with scenery designed to sustain the illusion of a "real" fairyland—with live animals running about. Oscar Asche, in his *As You Like It* of 1907, used moss-grown logs, 2,000 pots of fern, clumps of bamboo and cartloads of leaves from the previous autumn. Such performances were designed to suggest to actor and audience alike that they were sharing in "the real thing". Brecht believed this to be fatal to the art of the stage. The Alienation Effect is the sum total of technical means whereby the actor and audience are enabled to achieve this freedom from illusion of emotional authenticity and realism. The aim of Brecht's theatrical technique is to appeal less to the audience's emotion than to his reason. This may seem difficult to accept; we have been brought up on the notion that the theatre is the place where hearts are worn on the sleeve and everything is larger than life. We have been so accustomed to this form of day-dreaming in the theatre that one has to make a deliberate effort to dissociate oneself from set habits. Hence Brecht had thought out several ways of sharpening the spectator's critical awareness.

This is not the occasion to enter into a discussion of this technique. It will be enough to say that Robert Bolt himself has paid tribute to Brecht as a master mind whose influence on this play has been considerable:

> In two previous plays, *Flowering Cherry* and *The Tiger and the Horse*, I had tried, but with fatal timidity, to handle contemporaries in a style that should make them larger than life...Inevitably these plays looked like what they most resembled. [Mr Bolt here alludes to the theory that the theatre is a house with a fourth wall removed, so exposing all private action to view.] The style I eventually used was a bastardized version of the one most recently associated with Bertolt Brecht.

Then Bolt goes on to explain that many people have obtained a wrong idea of Brecht's theories. They regard the Alienation Effect as something like a "slap in the face". They think that alienation terminates rather than deepens audience participation. This is not so:

> Simply to slap your audience in the face satisfies an austere and puritanical streak which runs in many of his [Brecht's] disciples and sometimes, detrimentally I think, in Brecht himself. But it is a dangerous game to play...When we use alienation methods just for kicks we in the theatre are sawing through the branch on which we are sitting.

The most notorious of Brecht's alienation effects was the presence on the stage of a character who stood apart from the rest; here again Brecht was only building on the work of his predecessors in the theatre. Both the French stage of Dumas, and the theatre of Isben were perfectly familiar with the character of the Raisonneur—that is, a character who explains to the audience precisely what the problem is. Indeed perhaps the origin of the role goes back to Shakespearian times, when the first Gentleman, Second Gentleman and so on existed simply in order to lay bare antecedent events;

but the difference between Brecht and the eighteenth-century playwright who introduced "Charles, the hero's friend" in order to clear up all the points that required clearing up is that Brecht's method is to use the character not as a means of presenting expository material, but to address the audience direct, and so destroy the cosy illusion of naturalistic realism. The Common Man is a Brechtian protagonist cut down to size. "He is intended to draw the audience into the play, not thrust them off it." But the playwright considers himself largely to have failed in his intention—and for this reason. "The word '*common*' was intended primarily to indicate '*that which is common to us all*'. But he has taken instead as—that mythical beast The Man In The Street."

The result was that The Common Man divided the audience, in a sense politically, into opponents and supporters of the principle of egalitarianism. Some spectators assumed that the Common Man *was* common—and regarded him as vulgar. By others the role was resented as an attempt to divide mankind into "them" (representing the "Establishment") and "us"; a form of "U and non-U", to use Nancy Mitford's description.

Actually his chief contribution to the action of the play is that he proves invaluable in defining the various localities of episodes. Through the device of a wardrobe basket, containing appropriate costumes and "properties", he takes the opportunity to paint the scene and comment briefly on the action. Thus in the opening scene he assumes the character of More's steward Matthew, the arch-spokesman of common sense. From then on throughout the play, he assumes a number of small supporting parts—boatman, gaoler, executioner—in which his attitude is that of ironic commentator—the one man who has no illusions—and in that way the commentator constantly reminds the average audience of worldly-wise philosophy. His changes with the tide of circumstances, public opinion and private opportunity also serve to throw into relief the constant integrity of More.

The Duke

The Duke of Norfolk represents the aristocrats—the real rulers of the country. Actually he was Thomas, the eighth Duke of Norfolk (1473—1554). A life-long opponent of Wolsey, he might be taken as a symbol of the class which reflected the hatred of the nobles against self-made men, such as Wolsey, who achieved power without the need for influence. Whereas Wolsey was a poor man's son, a fact which rankles in Norfolk's heart, Norfolk symbolised all that wealth and privilege offered. In effect he was one of the last representatives of the baronial class, of whom Henry VIII had already disposed. Instead of turning to this class for running the country, Henry VIII put his trust in men like Wolsey and Cromwell, men without family connections, who therefore were committed exclusively to Henry's policies; they had been made by Henry, and were identified with his rule. They owed no allegiance to the Norfolks and their like, and that was why Norfolk displayed such a deep hatred of Wolsey, the arch-type of statesman who had taken over from the ruling families and threatened their existence. These enemies stood for opposite things; Norfolk's chief ambition was the ruin of Wolsey. And in the hour of Wolsey's downfall was the hour of Norfolk's triumph: hollow, for he did not succeed, as he had hoped, to Wolsey's fortunes. As President of the Privy Council he sought to replace Wolsey in the counsels of the King, but since he was destitute of Wolsey's genius he clearly could be of no great political service to him. Anne Boleyn was his niece; he watched her rise and fall with equal nonchalance. He presided over the trial which resulted in her being attainted for treason. But he had good luck with other relatives—another niece, Catherine Howard, became one of Henry's wives. Cromwell succeeded Wolsey as the real man of power, and Norfolk was merely a figure-head. It is this aspect of character which Bolt has seized upon for theatrical representation. He is perhaps the nearest to a "stock character"—says all the "right" things and holds the proper opinions for one of the country's "natural rulers", a typical figure of the Establishment who regards the country as his natural inheritance.

Thomas Cromwell

Bolt regards Thomas Cromwell as an intellectual bully. In the play, Cromwell had not then attained to the pinnacle of his career—when for six years he was the unmistakable ruler of Tudor England: but at any rate he both suggested and organised Henry's power. He is a rather terrifying figure; and Bolt sees him as something of a sadist, something of a power addict. He is vindictive (*e.g.* removing the books from More's prison cell) and sarcastic. The two qualities often go together. After the downfall of Cardinal Wolsey (because he failed to bring about the divorce), Henry found in Cromwell (1485—1544) a minister fitted to his ambition. Like Wolsey, Cromwell was a man of the humblest birth. He was the first layman actually to attain the greatest power in the state; an utter absence of moral scruple gives colour to the suggestion that he was an earnest disciple of Machiavelli. Indeed, in the play, it was he who recommended Rich to read Machiavelli. He is an expert in double talk and slippery tactics. Efforts have been made by some historians to evaluate Cromwell to the figure of a Protestant martyr, in view of his end. But such distortions of history have little effect. As A.D. Innes (*Ten Tudor Statesmen*) has written, "No playwright or novelist has made him a central figure in drama or novel. Yet it may seriously be argued that his personality was one which most decisively altered the course of history".

He was a man of action. Quite early in public life he poured contempt on "empty gabblers, who talked at large about everything under the sun while doing nothing". He was the first of the anti-Parliamentarians—the first of the Fascists. He came to the notice of Wolsey, and his affairs prospered. While the toils of the divorce suit gradually wore Wolsey down, and eventually brought about his downfall, Cromwell waited for his hour to strike. He obtained the ear of the King: finance was the keynote to his success. He struck at the authority of the Pope through the wealthy monasteries. It was Cromwell who promoted the Supremacy Bill; Wolsey's death had proved most convenient; his successor was Cranmer, a sufficiently pliable tool without qualms of conscience.

In the play momentous events seem to happen with the inevitability of a dream. Dates are not important, but 1533 is important in that it saw the irreversible breach with the Papacy, although in fact it was not until 1534 that Pope Clement issued judgment in favour of Catherine. From that moment King Henry and Cromwell went ahead. The marriage with Anne Boleyn led to the Act of Succession. "I pray that these things be not confirmed with oaths", said More. But that is exactly what happened.

To force both More and Fisher to acknowledge the Royal Supremacy in place of the Pope's would have been the supreme triumph. Nothing would have beaten down possible opposition so much as the winning over of such opponents. Cromwell drafted the Oath in such a way that there was no escaping by means of legal quibbles. More and Fisher refused to desert their principles. They would accept the succession as a pragmatic measure—a *fait accompli*; they would never take the Oath as prescribed.

It is important for the student to understand the exact position; in the theatre events take place so quickly that the spectator has not time to grasp the significance of the issues involved, and in so far as this happens the play is less successful dramatically. He may imagine that More and Fisher were making a mountain out of a mole-hill.

Nothing could be further from the truth. Both Cromwell and Henry were anxious to proceed according to the strict letter of the law. Yet it appeared that mere refusal to take the Oath—silence, malicious or otherwise—offered a defence; the omission was soon rectified. A new Treason Act was passed, in which it was expressly declared treason merely to question the titles of the Queen and her heirs, and silence was to be construed as treason.

It was this that brought More and Fisher within the net. If they remained firm, there was no escape from execution.

We do not know for sure, but it is possible that Henry might have allowed More, out of regard for happy days long past, to spend his days in prison. We do not know: it is just possible. There is not the slightest shadow of doubt that Cromwell did not suffer a single qualm. But the death sentence was made certain when the new Pope, who succeeded Clement, created Fisher a Cardinal. To Cromwell these men had been merely obstacles; to Henry they now appeared as implacable enemies. More's doom was thus sealed.

The Archbishop

Thomas Cranmer (1489—1556) was a rather dim figure; against his will he was compelled to be a protagonist in a drama which he neither understood nor wanted. Few characters have aroused as much controversy as Cranmer, and Bolt, not surprisingly, has taken refuge in a rather conventional portrait of a stage-figure instead of stating an original viewpoint. It is somewhat difficult to form any view of this rather colourless figure: certainly the stage Cranmer shows little sign of the man who aroused such bitter controversy among his biographers. Historically, every important action in Cranmer's life has had its defenders and its attackers. A very interesting character, he makes little impression in this play. That he held no strong views on the Papacy we may well believe. His career was undistinguished in the sense that he apparently did little to deserve the greatness that was thrust upon him. Whereas More instantly made his mark felt, Cranmer spent twenty-five years in an inferior position at Cambridge. His chance came with the "king's affair"—the great divorce. Cranmer made an original contribution to the theological question: and Henry thus discovered the man who "had the sow by the right ear". He distinguished himself as a propagandist for the King's cause and he wrote a book on the divorce—written in the hospitality of the house of Anne Boleyn's father. As it transpired Pope Clement gave an adverse judgment before Cranmer had an opportunity of raising the technical points involved in a consideration of *Deuteronomy* and *Leviticus*.

By practice men become masters of intrigue. The Cambridge recluse in course of time became a cunning and skilful agent on behalf of his king. His connection with the Boleyn interest thrived, and he received his reward in 1533 when he was appointed Archbishop of Canterbury. (Incidentally, the precise chronology of the play is not always clear. Act One ended in 1530; Act Two begins in May 1532. But the exact timing of each individual episode is left indefinite. It is not necessary for a comprehension of the play to allocate the date of these scenes exactly.)

Certainly he tried to persuade More that Catherine of Aragon's marriage was invalid (More being Lord Chancellor at that time). His appointment as Archbishop was unexpected, at any rate no one outside the Royal Circle knew of the high opinion that Henry had formed of Cranmer. The fact is that the powerful influence of the Boleyn family had been at work. But to the ordinary "man in the street" it looked as though this was simple trading. Cranmer seemed to have said in effect, "Make me the Archbishop of Canterbury, and I will give you leave to be an adulterer".

Although seemingly a somewhat colourless figure, nevertheless Cranmer did put his finger on one of the weaknesses of More's case. If More did not blame those who took the Oath of Supremacy, it *must* be that it was doubtful. In the case of doubt, he ought to give the benefit to Henry. His was the only argument that baffled More: he could think of no answer.

Richard Rich

Rich was an almost exact contemporary of Roper, and in the play represents the "younger generation". Although unfamiliar to all except students doing research in the Tudor period, Richard Rich was the typical turn-coat, the man who benefits from kindness, and then takes great pleasure in biting the hand that has fed him. Practically all the men who played a great part in Henry's reign, Wolsey, More, Fisher, Cromwell, Somerset, Seymour, all sooner or later went to the block. Rich, the Judas of English history, alone died safely in his bed.

The playwright has presented him as a "studious unhappy academic, tortured by doubt, longing to be rescued from himself". This would appear to be a very subjective interpretation, the actual Rich being a much more detestable figure—but a figure which every despotism throws up, the figure who contrives to keep a safe skin while his betters go under.

He is introduced as a struggling barrister, a Cambridge man who is recommended to go in for teaching—More is prepared to find him a post with Dr. Colet of St. Paul's. But Rich is prepared to work only for self-advancement and therefore thinks it more expedient to fawn upon his social betters, More, Cromwell and Wolsey. His career began when he came to the notice of Wolsey: like many reactionaries in later life, he began by being a wholesale reformer who smelt out corruption in high places. In May 1532 he was made Attorney General for Wales, the first of the plums of office that fell into his lap. The dramatist has used some license in incorporating historical facts: in October 1533 he was knighted on becoming Solicitor General, and it was in that capacity he took the leading part in More's prosecution for treason.

It was his perjured evidence that ultimately convicted More. Rich reaped the reward—he was loaded with money and honours. In one of his "Establishment"speeches he once likened Henry VIII to a Solomon for justice, a Samson for strength and an Absalom for handsomeness; nor did he run out of metaphors there, for he added a Sun without which life could not exist. Next to Cromwell he was the most powerful of the "Establishment" but with this difference: he always managed to be on the winning side, in spite of the many changes of mood and policy of his master Henry.

When Cromwell, too, fell on evil times, Rich, rat-like, deserted the sinking ship; repeating the pattern of his perjury in the More trial, he turned against Cromwell at the last, in what Froude described as "The darkest page in England's history". It has been said that "the roll of martyrs in England was due to Rich's persecution".

The part of Rich is somewhat under-played by Bolt and the playwright has sought fit to whitewash the character of a man who merited the universal condemnation of posterity.

Historically his only act of benevolence was the founding of Felsted public school. Rich is a typical instrument of tyranny, the pliant and willing instrument, a type of which the world has had many examples in recent years. His perjured character throws More's integrity into strong dramatic relief. It was More's individual integrity ("selfhood" Bolt calls it) coupled with Rich's perjury that sent More to his death.

William Roper

William Roper was the son-in-law of Sir Thomas More, who married

Answers.

More's daughter (by his first wife) Margaret. He is envisaged in this play as a man in his early thirties— a man of little imagination, but consumed with rectitude and principle: he was historically, the first biographer of the saint of "clear and unspotted conscience". He was continually resident in More's household and it is largely through his *Life* that we know more of More's household, his background and personal environment than is usual in the case of great men. The play undoubtedly owes a great deal to Roper's biography, which must have been one of the dramatist's primary sources.

He is first introduced to the audience as a suitor for the hand of Margaret, although More at the beginning is against the proposed marriage. With Rich, Roper represents the younger generation (a better specimen); like Rich he has been reading for the bar, and when he enters the play, he is about to be called. As More says, the Ropers were barristers when the Mores were selling pewter, but More's objection to Roper as a son-in-law is not based on family fortune, it is simply that Roper is a heretic, a Lutheran; maybe it is only the natural idealism of young men, but More is determined that until Roper changes his ideas he shall not marry Margaret. As it happens Roper changes his allegiance, and when Henry attacks the Church, Roper in his idealism supports the Pope. He says to Margaret, "I'm not a convenient man, Meg—I've got an inconvenient conscience!" More laughingly likens him to Joshua's trumpet—"One note on that brass conscience of yours and my daughter's walls are down." He clearly is no time-server, and he is not afraid to tell More to his face that "The Court has corrupted you, Sir Thomas; you are not the man you were; you have learnt to study your '*convenience*'; you have learnt to flatter!"

Roper is not a "trimmer"—he will not win Margaret by sacrificing his independence. In this respect he is a complete foil to Rich. And there is a brief, but valuable scene of confrontation between Roper and Rich in which Roper is quick to detect Rich's defection.

In certain respects he is more alive to the dangers of More's position than More himself seems to be. At any rate he realises the logical consequences of Henry's Act of Supremacy earlier than More does; he cuts through the mumbo-jumbo of legalism and straightway maintains that the legal quibble on which More is content to rely at first will prove useless. Like many a man of strong principle he is a nuisance to those around him, a constant reminder of the pure and holy—he will not be discreet. Yet when Alice is resentful at More's refusal to keep in with the powers that be, it is to Roper that he turns for comfort.

Roper is not a superficial man, and is rather inclined to frown on More's habit of self-mockery at important moments—"While we are witty", he says quietly, "the Devil may enter us unawares." It is Roper who brings the information that there is to be a new Act of Parliament requiring everyone to take an Oath, failure to take which is to be construed as treason. More is quick to ask, "But what is the wording?" Roper contemptuously replies they are concerned with meaning not words. But More, anxious to find a place to rest a possible defence, says that an oath consists of words. Here one feels that Roper was right in the larger sense; he is not to be put off by a narrow legalistic defence.

The King

It is important to realise that this play is a play about More, not primarily about Henry VIII. This King has passed into the mythology of the English race, and he is remembered in history as a gross sensualist who combined insatiable tyranny and bestial appetites in about equal proportions. In the play he is important as the dictator whose actions and policy (carried out by his underlings) are responsible for More's dilemma. Henry appears only in one scene. In this scene he appears not as the over-fed outsize of Holbein's portrait, but rather as a young king always talking about himself, delighted as a ten-year-old to get his shoes muddy, unwarrantably proud of his skill in dancing and wrestling and of his flimsy accomplishments ("we artists") very well satisfied that he is in a position to command better men than himself and losing his temper as soon as he is crossed. He is not altogether pleased when his knowledge of Latin is surpassed. Although pleased to be commended as a writer, when his ability in Latin is shown to be secondary he petulantly deprecates books and learning by quoting a Bible tag. In all accomplishments he shall be the first. However, he soon recovers to announce to Margaret that "I'm something of a scholar too". He likes people to hang on his words and goes on talking of what he has been doing even while music is playing and when he has commanded More to listen to it ("*Listen*, man, *listen*"). "I launched a ship today, Thomas," he goes on, quite certain that he will have no competition in conversation. His own selfish nature as an absolute monarch, coupled with other people's flattery, has made him into a most contemptible character and leads on to the final scene of the play.

Eustace Chapuys

Chapuys was the Ambassador in England of King Charles V of Spain, Holy Roman Emperor. A man of some sixty years of age, he is represented in the play as a somewhat ridiculous intriguer. As suits his diplomatic status, he endeavours to stand much on his dignity. Chapuys appears to possess a fair degree of native shrewdness, although he seriously underestimates the honesty of More's character. According to the playwright, he "trots happily along a mental footpath as narrow as a peasant's".

Lady Alice More

Lady Alice, More's second wife, was the widow of John Middleton, a London merchant. A woman of scant education, she belonged to a different sphere of society than her husband. However, she proved to be a good housewife and step-mother, albeit something of a shrew.

Her character in the play is true to life. She had little appreciation of More's difficulties, and was clearly resentful of the misfortunes which resulted from his struggle with the King.

However, as she herself tells us (Act II, Seventh Scene), she is fully aware of his nobility of spirit, even while she deplores the fact that he appears bent on self-sacrifice. There is no doubt of the affection which each feels for the other.

Lady Margaret More

Margaret More, known as Lady Margaret by courtesy, was More's favourite daughter. Eventually to become the wife of William Roper, Margaret was a woman of outstanding character and intellect. A bluestocking, capable of disputing philosophy and of speaking and writing Latin and Greek as well as any scholar of her period, she was nevertheless a woman of lively and sympathetic disposition.

She is perhaps best remembered for the affection that she displayed towards her father, especially during the period of his imprisonment. As depicted in the play, she is entirely true to life.

Cardinal Wolsey (1475—1530)

Wolsey, a commoner by birth, was the son of a butcher or grazier. Taking Holy Orders as a young man, he rose rapidly by virtue of his undoubted ability from one office to another.

His association with the Royal Family began when he became Chaplain to Henry VII. In 1511 he was appointed to the household of Henry VIII, and in 1513 became a Privy Councillor. He eventually combined in his own person the functions of Lord Chancellor, Archbishop of York, and Cardinal Legate.

For some fourteen years before his death, he was, at the King's pleasure, the virtual ruler of England. As Lord Chancellor, he maintained close control of the Ecclesiastical Courts, in the Star Chamber he curbed the activities of the nobility, while in the Court of Requests he brought cheap legal remedies within the reach of the poor. No public man of his day accumulated more offices or wielded more power.

Indeed, he was a man obsessed by the lust for power, and was apparently governed by few other considerations. His private life was lax, and he was notoriously neglectful of his pastoral duties. A villain and upstart in the eyes of many, he was nevertheless regarded as a hero by some.

Wolsey fell from power as a result of his failure to arrange a speedy divorce for King Henry VIII. Furious at the long and slow proceedings being undertaken by Wolsey and Cardinal Campeggio, who together constituted a Papal Court , and the fact that the Pope suddenly transferred the hearing from England to Italy, the King at first stripped Wolsey of his political powers and a good deal of his personal property. Some few months afterwards, he was recalled from the Archbishopric of York, to which he had been banished, on charges of High Treason. Wolsey died of illness at Leicester, while on his way to the Tower of London to face these charges.

The playwright's reconstruction of Wolsey appears to be within the bounds of historical accuracy. He is depicted as an old man who "now inhabits a lonely den of self-indulgence and contempt." During his interview with More in Act I, Sixth Scene, it is entirely evident that the Cardinal fears the consequences, should his efforts fail to result in a divorce for the King.

In the play, as in life, Wolsey makes little effort to conceal the fact that he is a man of few scruples. He conceives it to be his duty to carry out the wishes of the King, his master, quite irrespective of the principles involved.

The Metamorphic Structure Of *A Man For All Seasons*

In his preface to *A Man For All Seasons*[1] Robert Bolt relates that one of his intentions as a playwright is to construct a " '*bold and beautiful verbal architecture*' " (xvii), not unlike a poem in that metaphor and imagery are consciously employed (xv). In "Robert Bolt: Self, Shadow, and the Theatre of Recognition, "[2] Anselm Atkins has already discussed Bolt's use of the structural dialectic that may be seen in considering the relationship between Sir Thomas More and the Common Man—which results in a synthesis of apposite and opposite points necessary to the success of any kind of "architecture." My purpose here is to examine another aspect of Bolt's craftsmanship: his use of metaphor to reinforce the theme of conflict between More's selfhood and the demands of Henry's England.

Bolt discusses in his preface why he chooses to use the particular metaphors that he does and what effect he hopes to achieve:

> I know no other way to treat this subject. In the play I used a poetic image. As a figure for the superhuman context I took the largest, most alien, least formulated thing I know, the sea and water. The references to ships, rivers, currents, tides, navigation, and so on, are all used for this purpose. Society by contrast figures as dry land. I set out with no very well-formed idea of the kind of play it was to be, except that it was not to be naturalistic. The possibility of using imagery, that is of using metaphors not decoratively but with an intention, was a side effect of that.(xv)

Bolt goes on to say that no one seemed to notice what he did, but he also notes that "it's the nature of imagery to work, in performance at any rate, unconsciously." (xv) Bolt does create in his play the atmosphere necessary for the audience's appreciation—conscious or unconscious—of the significant actions of the plot. But the "superhuman context" that Bolt creates through use of metaphor looms even larger when the significance of the land-water imagery is consciously perceived upon a more critical scrutiny than would be made in the theater.

As a metaphor, water is used in three distinct ways in *A Man For All Seasons*. First, as Bolt notes, varied references to it provide overall a cosmic background for More's adamant resolution to be true to his self in the conflict that he is engaged in. Working in conjunction with the characters of the play, who exhibit a less pronounced moral stature than More and thus serve the function of the foil, the indefinite and "least formulated" sea imagery assists in the magnification of More's stance as the hero; even if on the unconscious level it is a dramatically successful device.

The second way in which water is used as metaphor is much more definite and specifically meaningful to the theme of the play. For, as the land metaphor represents society—society being clearly defined and formulated by law, which is "the very pattern of society" (xiv)—in the play, the water's indefiniteness comes to be identified with the subjective quantity that More terms his self. More uses this metaphor for his selfhood when his daughter, Meg, pleads with him in prison to "say the words of the oath and in your heart think otherwise." (81) More, performing an action which has the religious overtones of the sacramental consecration in the Roman Catholic Mass, answers Meg thus:

> When a man takes an oath, Meg, he's holding his own self in his hands. Like water. (*He cups his hands*) And if he opens his fingers *then*—he needn't hope to find himself again. Some men aren't capable of this, but I'd be loath to think your father one of them. (81)

It is a substance not open to objective delineation that More holds, as is evidenced by Norfolk's inability to understand when More states that "what matters to me is not whether it's [apostolic succession] true or not but that I believe it to be true, or rather, not that I *believe* it, but that *I* believe it." (53)[3] In attempting to explain his notion of selfhood to Alice, More poses as close a definition as he can: "there's a little...little, area...where I must rule myself. It's very little—less to him [Henry] than a tennis court." (34) However, the overwhelming importance of this self is judged by More as paramount to life itself. Later, Norfolk unwittingly recalls the water-self metaphor and reinforces its significance in terms of More's evaluation of it by stating to More at his trial: "your life lies in your own hand, Thomas, as it always has." (87)

With water as a metaphor for selfhood, the logical question to ask of the play is how the conflict between selfhood and Henry's society, between the water and land metaphors, is expressed. The situation is expressed metaphorically in the mode that might be expected: the result is mud.

More's steadfast position is representative of that which is sanctioned by genuine civil and religious law, as More clearly explains in his speech at the court room after having been betrayed by Rich's perjury. (92-93) In marked contrast is Henry's unlawful decision to put away Catherine for the sake of having Anne for his wife. By definition, Henry as a Renaissance king is representative of the entire society; thus More's legally sanctioned selfhood is counterposed to Henry's—and by implication, society's[4]—selfish desire to pervert the law in order to fit his own whims. The result is an *erosion* of English law and society. The expression of this through the mud metaphor is first encountered when More is meeting with Wolsey on the subject of Henry's divorce. During the meeting Henry returns from a visit to Anne, and Wolsey tells More that "he's been to play in the mud again." (12) Later, when Henry visits More at Chelsea, he greets More and states: "I happened to be on the river. (*Holds out shoe, proudly*) Look, mud." (27)[5]

By the time of the visit of More's family to his prison cell, the dissolution of the "land" has occurred throughout Henry's realm. In this scene the Jailer, one of the lowest on the societal hierarchy, attempts to remove Alice from the cell and is told: "*Don't* put your muddy hand on me!" (84) Henry's destruction of genuine law, the law which More thought would protect his life is complete. Hence, when More is finally brought to trial, the mud metaphor is replaced by one that more intensely expresses what has happened. It is, appropriately enough, Cromwell who uses the new metaphor when entering the court room. He states:

> So, now we'll apply to good, plain sailor's art
> And fix these quicksands on the Law's plain chart. (86)

Henry and his society are expressed in terms of the result of the conflict between true selfhood and corrupted society, between the water metaphor and the eroded land. More stands as the fixed point and does not cause the destruction of order that goes on about him; that is, he is never directly associated with the mud metaphor as is Henry. It is Henry who starts the process of erosion; for Henry, like More, realizes what it means to have a self, a soul or conscience, as More points out. (68) More eventually becomes trapped in the "quicksands" at his trial only because Henry had already "opened his hands" and let his selfhood escape by the time of More's visit to Wolsey. Hence, the primary sigificance of the mud is the contrast between More's retention of self and Henry's loss of it. Selfhood, and the degree to which a character maintains it, is an integral part of the theme of the play; and More dramatically emerges as the constant, the "hero of selfhood" (xiii), to which all must be referred when the standards of the society are destroyed.

The water-self metaphor is one aspect of the metaphoric structure of *A Man for All Seasons*. It is an essential one in that it expresses the real presence of the individual conscience and the fact that moral and immoral actions result from its functioning and malfunctioning. Consequently, Bolt sets up a standard which negates the possibility of a strictly naturalistic interpretation of the historical event of More's destruction.

Bolt goes to great pains in his preface to point out that the drama of Sir Thomas More *might* very well be treated in a naturalistic fashion, that is, as the necessary result of the coalescence of various political, economic, religious, and social forces operating at that particular time in history. Indeed, all might be written-off to the environmental factors of sixteenth-century England, if individuals had not precipitated the necessary actions. Bolt explains the reasons for the way he did decide to treat the situation of More, and the reasons for not treating it naturalistically thus:

> The economy was very progressive, the religion was very

> reactionary. We say therefore that the collision was inevitable, setting Henry aside as a colorful accident. With Henry presumably we set aside as accidents Catherine and Wolsey and Anne and More and Cranmer and Cromwell and the Lord Mayor of London and the man who washed his windows; setting indeed everyone aside as an accident, we say that the collision was inevitable. But that, on reflection, seems only to say that it happened. What is of interest is the way it happened, the way it was lived. For lived such collisions are. (ix)

The subject of Bolt's play, therefore, is the way in which the free agents, the "selves," within the multi-faceted environment of Henry's England act and react to one another and the environment that is created in the course of these actions.

Bolt depicts his characters in their individual moral choices and actions; but he also provides a metaphor for the situation they create and are influenced by. Bolt's choice for the metaphor is the river, the third way in which water is used as a metaphor. With the incessant flow of the river, and the relationships of the characters to this metaphor, Bolt expresses the "collision" that became "inevitable".

Act II begins with the Common Man making this explicit identification of the river with the actions that have occurred during the two year interim since the close of Act I. Holding a history of England, he addresses the audience thus:

> Two years. During that time a lot of water's flowed under the bridge, and one of the things that have come floating along is ... (*Reads*) "The Church of England....Only an unhappy few were found to set themselves against the current of the times, and in doing so court disaster." (47)

"The current of the times" is the most apt description of the series of events that the river signifies. The characters of the play have contributed to its nature (recall that Henry has "opened his hands") and thus interpret and act accordingly to it in different ways. Machiavellian Cromwell sees it as an obscure force that determines men's fates. He tells Rich, "It's odd how men's fortunes flow. My late master, Wolsey, died in disgrace and here I am in the king's own service." (21) Accordingly, Cromwell, while realizing the danger of doing so, goes with the current of the times for the sake of self-aggrandizement. Yet, because he does realize that he is engaged in a dangerous game, he realistically views the situation as possibly destructive. Deviousness and manipulation of the law are profitable, but Cromwell keeps his eye on a possible means of escape for when the flow of events may necessitate it. His employment of perjury as a means to preserve his political life is foreshadowed as plausible in one of Cromwell's early discussions with Rich:

> RICH. There are some things one wouldn't do for anything. Surely.

CROMWELL. Mm—that idea's like these life lines they have on the embankment: comforting, but you don't expect to use them (41)

Perjury does become the "life line" for Cromwell and Rich when they must save themselves from Henry's impatience. (79)

This method of describing the characters' situations by reference to the river is repeated over and over again. Shortly before going over to Cromwell's side, Rich pleads with More for an honorable position, crying "I'm adrift. Help me." (37) The Common Man, as Steward, had earlier expressed his creed that "the great thing's not to get out of your depth" (24); but one by one, the characters place actions which come together with others and form the historical force that the river represents. Once these actions are placed and begin to coalesce, the characters come under the influence of the sum of all the actions which roll toward the conclusion of the play. In short, the characters get out of their depths.

Even Henry becomes bound inextricably, despite the possibility of choosing to terminate the trend of events, to the sequence of actions he has initiated by his decision to consort with Anne. This phenomenon is poignantly portrayed by Bolt when Henry takes his new ship, the *Great Harry*, on its maiden voyage. Arriving at More's home, Henry loudly boasts of his expertise as a sailor: "I steered her, Thomas, under sail" (29); "I shall not forget the feel of that ... great tiller under my hands." (30) But, although Henry wears the garb of a legitimate pilot and even has an authentic pilot's whistle, which he childishly blows upon when making his regal entrance at Chelsea, the notion that Henry is less than in full control on the river gradually emerges. It may be recalled that, prior to Henry's trip to Chelsea, Cromwell had told Chapuys that Henry "will have assistance, of course" (22) in his steering of the *Great Harry*.

Henry's self-satisfied description of his sailing skills to More is frequently interrupted by lengthy pleas for More to sanction his desire to wed Anne and put away Catherine. It is a volition that determines his actions; and, although Henry states, "There's the road for me, Thomas, the river; my river" (27), it becomes clear that the currents he originally initiated have come to exercise a binding influence on him. For instance, when More tells Henry the time, Henry is compelled to depart, saying:

> Eight o'clock you said? Thomas, the tide will be changing. I was forgetting the tide. I'd better go....I must catch the tide or I'll not get back to Richmond till...No, don't come...Oh, Lady Alice, I must go....I want to catch the tide. To tell the truth, Lady Alice, I have forgotten in your haven here how time flows past outside. Affairs call me to court and so I give you my thanks and say good night. (33)

One of the "affairs" at court that draws Henry away is Anne's habit of dancing at eight o'clock. (34) This is a part of the "tide" of the river that exercises a sense of compulsion on Henry.

Another character who is described in relationship with the river is

Roper, whose moral fickleness is sharply contrasted with More's steadfastness. More's uneasiness at Roper's vacillating position is

> Will, I'd trust you with my life. But not your principles. (*They mount the stairs*) You speak of being anchored to our principles. But if the weather turns nasty you up with the anchor and let it down where there's less wind, and fishing better. And "Look," we say, "look, I'm anchored." (39)

Roper's erratic changes in moral perspectives certainly verify More's view of his "seagoing principles"(38); but more important to the metaphoric structure of the play, the figure of Roper as an aimless boatman on the river serves to effectively point out the situation of More, as More views it, in relation to the stream of events. More believes that he, unlike Roper, is safely anchored to the land, that is, the laws and their protection, through the means of silence on Henry's actions. Like Cromwell, he believes that there is always a life line to the refuge of the land when the current of the river becomes too strong; hence, it is the "thickets of the law"(37) that More persists in believing in as an ultimate place of safety. In explaining the refuge that silence can provide, More tells Alice in language that echoes Cromwell's that "It's only a life line, we shan't have to use it but it's comforting to have." (56) Unfortunately, Cromwell's "life line" (41) of perjury and More's of legal protection through silence are diametrically opposed, and the basis for More's trust in his life line is undermined.

The river functions as a central metaphor in the exposition of the theme of More's struggle for survival with integrity, and throughout *A Man For All Seasons* there is a metaphorical voyage of More toward that point at which Cromwell will employ his life line and destroy More. The motif begins when More is first called to Wolsey. It is a boat trip on the river that he takes to Richmond. On the voyage back to Chelsea, after refusing to support Wolsey, More sails on a river that has begun "tilting up" (16); and, at this particular time when the events leading up to More's death are initiated, the Boatman remarks that there is a channel in the middle of the river that is "getting deeper all the time." (16) By the time that More sails to Richmond in order to answer the charges of Cromwell, the river has carried him to the point at which he is stranded from his "haven" at Chelsea. Events have placed him in a position from which there is no return, as More indicates when Cromwell reads a condemnatory letter from Henry.

> MORE. ...So I am brought here at last.
> CROMWELL. Brought? You brought yourself to where you stand now.
> MORE. Yes—still, in another sense—I was brought.
> CROMWELL. Oh, yes. You may go home now. (68-69).

But More cannot "go home" by way of the river; at this point, the direction of events in the situation is irreversible. The river is no longer navigable for More, and when he calls for transportation, it is not forthcoming:

> Boat!...Boat!...*(to himself)* Oh, come along. it's not as bad as that....(*Calls*) Boat! (69).

The fact that More is divorced from the way in which Henry's world is moving is further emphasized when, waiting for a boat, he meets Norfolk, who exclaims that "the one fixed point in a world of changing friendships is that Thomas More will not give in!" (70) More is a fixed point, morally separated from the realities of Henry's England, and from Cromwell's point of view, he is "a man who raises a gale and won't come out of the harbor." (69) Acquiescence to the realities of society means the surrender of his integral selfhood, and More remains aloof.

As the play progresses, the river comes to take on a sinister character of its own in terms of its relationship to More. More, who is "easily seasick...and afraid of drowning" according to the Boatman (24), sees the river as "very black" (16) when leaving from his interview with Wolsey in Act I. It becomes the medium in which Cromwell and Rich set their "net" (60) for More; and it is highly significant that, prior to going to Cromwell's inquiry, More tells Roper that his case is "watertight." (65)

The river's final significance is strikingly drawn when More and his family quietly discuss the bleak condition of his prison cell:

> ROPER. This is an awful place!
> MORE. Except it's keeping me from you, my dears, it's not so bad. Remarkably like any other place.
> ALICE. (*Looks up critically*) It drips!
> MORE. Yes. Too near the river. (80)

This brief scene provides a condensed, and immediately engaging, picture of the total alienation of More from the life activities of Henry's world. The by now omnipresent river runs by him as he remains immovably fixed to his personal position.[6] Thus, it is bitterly ironical, yet perfectly fitting, that Cromwell should enter the court room for More's trial poetically praising the law as a "Great Ship." (85-86) It sails on Henry's river, past More, and like everything and everyone that is a part of the play, it has come to the same end, a sordid loss of genuineness.

With the river expressing a malign force created by the actions of Henry and his followers, with the erosion of the land metaphor signifying the dissolution of the legal guarantees of a moral and orderly society, the play moves forward through its series of events to its logical end. Thus, through the use of metaphor, Bolt has established a series of leitmotifs which dramatically informs and illuminates the plot of the play. The extended metaphors of land, water, river, and river voyage, whether working unconsciously on the audience or consciously described, give to *A Man For All Seasons* the dense richness that is a necessary characteristic of an artistically great play.

Bolt refers to his drama as "conventional" in an interview with Charles Marowitz, and the way in which Bolt explicates what is meant by that term speaks best for the effect that his use of metaphor has on his play. He states:

> Highly conventional theatre, where both sides of the footlights understand thoroughly what is going on, is like a drum-skin which is very, very tight. You tap it and it's resonant.[7]

It is a "resonance" that Bolt achieves in *A Man For All Seasons*. Each metaphorical sequence, reflecting figuratively the actions of the play, sounds its own note and echoes in unison with the others, stating and restating the theme. It is a " '*bold and beautiful verbal architecture*' " (xvii) that Robert Bolt creates; and if his metaphor may be extended, the acoustics are perfect.

By Joseph R. McElrath, Jr. From *Modern Drama* (May, 1971).

[1]Page references in the text of this paper will be to the Vintage Books edition (1962) of *A Man For All Seasons*.

[2]Anselm Atkins, "Robert Bolt: Self, Shadow, and the Theatre of Recognition," *Modern Drama*, X (1967), 182-188.

[3]In regard to his emphasis on the notion of *I* and his wish to communicate its meaning, More restates it later to Norfolk, employing at the same time a comparison of self with water. Adjusting his figures so as to effectively impress the somewhat thick-headed Norfolk, More says: "And what would you do with a water spaniel that was afraid of water? You'd hang it! Well, as a spaniel is to water, so is man to his own self. I will not give in because I oppose it—I do—not my pride, not my spleen, nor any of my appetites, but *I* do—*I*." (71)

[4]As More notes, the "subjects are associated with the actions of Kings willy-nilly." (49)

[5]Bolt gives fuller treatment to this action of Henry in his screenplay for the movie version of *A Man For All Seasons* by having Henry sink ankle-deep in the mud upon leaving his barge at Chelsea. Henry trudges through some ten or twenty yards of the stuff, self-consciously laughing at his unregal situation; significantly his courtiers follow suit.

[6]The intensity of More's isolation is further emphasized by two images which Alice employs on page 55. Alluding to the isolated state of the narrator in Eliot's *The Love Song of J. Alfred Prufrock*, Bolt has Alice declare to her daughter, "Oh, you'd walk on the bottom of the sea and think yourself a crab if he [More] suggested it." At the same time she recalls another of Eliot's images of isolation when she asks More, "Poor silly man, do you think they'll leave you here to learn to fish?"

[7]Kelly Morris, ed., "An Interview With Robert Bolt by Charles Marowitz," *TDR*, XI (1966), 139.

Review Questions and Answers

Question 1.

Discuss the attitudes of Henry VIII and his advisers towards reform within the Church.

Answer

With the accession of Henry VIII to the English throne in 1509, the devotees of the "New Learning" believed that a new era of social and religious enlightenment was about to dawn. The new king made some concessions to public sentiment by cancelling some of the financial obligations of those who, during the reign of his father, had been subjected to extortion in the interest of the public treasury. Moreover, Henry, who had supposedly absorbed some of the spirit of the Renaissance from his tutors, made his court the resort of men filled with the new beliefs.

Cardinal Wolsey, Henry's Chancellor, was sufficiently a realist to appreciate the need for modest reforms in the Church. He encouraged bishops and abbots to exercise stricter authority over their subordinates. He obtained from the Pope restrictions on the taking of minor Church orders, and later secured Papal authority to inspect the monasteries, some of which he dissolved, and others of which he drained in the interest of the royal purse.

However, in matters of doctrine, Henry displayed a determined aversion to reform. With the forthrightness of an absolute monarch, he fiercely opposed Luther's onslaught against the Papacy and the sanctity of Catholic doctrine and dogma. In 1521, the King published a pamphlet, *Assertion of the Seven Sacraments* in which he defended the supremacy of the Pope, and the sacraments of the Catholic Church. It was as a reward for this that Pope Leo X conferred upon him the style and title of "Defender of the Faith." But, in the light of subsequent events, the King's singlemindedness was not destined to endure.

When the matter of his divorce was being violently contested, he had fallen under the influence of a counsellor. Thomas Cromwell, a man of pronounced Protestant sympathies. Accordingly, at this man's instigation, a number of minor changes was brought about. These included the compulsory use of a Bible in English, the destruction of some supposedly miraculous images, the abolition of pilgrimages, and the condemnation of the sale of indulgences. The major change was the suppression of the English monasteries in 1536. Yet it may be assumed, that in this matter, the motive largely or partly financial, since much of the resultant treasure was given to the crown. But whatever his motives, the suppression of the monasteries met with a large measure of support, especially from the humanists and those with Protestant sympathies. Even to those most opposed to the measure, it was rendered tolerable by the financial endowment of schools and churches, the granting of livings and pensions to members of the dispossessed orders, and the transfer of much monastic property to territorial landowners.

The most dangerous opposition to the King's action against the monasteries came from the north of England, where attachment to tradition was stronger than elsewhere and where, moreover, the monasteries were of relatively high repute, and were of outstanding importance in their help and relief of an impoverished population. While the so-called Pilgrimage of Grace was vigorously suppressed, it served to warn the King to proceed no further along the road of anti-Catholicism.

The Ten Articles of 1536 and the Six Articles of 1539 contained little that was anti-Catholic in sentiment. At this stage, the King was pursuing a *via media*; his subjects were forbidden to pay allegiance to the Pope, while they were not permitted to be Lutherans. Supporters of either extreme were bitterly persecuted, and Thomas Cromwell himself, partly as a result of his support of Lutheran devotees, was executed in 1540.

While the King could hardly fail to be influenced by the Reformation in continental Europe, it is worthy of remark that he considered himself just as much a Catholic as he was before the separation from Rome. The notion to which the King clung was that the Church in England remained as it was, except that he, and not the Pope, was its head.

Question 2.

Discuss the events which led to the establishment of the Anglican Church.

Answer

Henry VIII, in furtherance of his design to strengthen England against the waxing power of France, resolved to ally his country with Spain. As a sign of his good faith, he entered into a contract by which Arthur, Prince of Wales, was married to Catherine, the daughter of Ferdinand and Isabella. Since Arthur died shortly thereafter, it was then decided that the widow Catherine should be married to Arthur's surviving brother, Henry. This latter step was taken despite the fact that, according to an ancient ecclesiastical law, a man was forbidden to marry his deceased brother's wife. However, the difficulty occasioned by the inconvenient "Law of Consanguinity" was overcome by the device of a special dispensation granted by Pope Julius II. Accordingly, in the year of Henry VIII's accession, the newly crowned king was married to Catherine of Aragon.

For some twenty years, the King, superficially at least, appeared to be devoted to his Queen, but gradually a change became manifest. By 1527 Catherine had given birth to several children, but only one, Princess Mary, had survived. It was apparently because the male succession to the throne was in doubt that Henry VIII began to ponder the question of divorce, and in 1527 he informed Cardinal Wolsey, his Chancellor, of this intention.

Since, according to Christian dogma, marriage is regarded as a sacrament, divorce was permitted only in the most exceptional circumstances. The King's case, in his own view, was exceptional, since he contended that the Papal dispensation which gave legal sanction to his marriage was in itself illegal, being counter to the "Law of Consanguinity." Accordingly, Cardinal Wolsey was charged with the duty of prevailing upon Pope Clement VII, to acknowledge the King's contention, the effect of which would have been to render his marriage with Catherine null and void. The Pope, however, displayed no eagerness to comply with Henry's suit. His reasons were, perhaps, two-fold; he may have been influenced by genuine scruples, and also by the desire not to offend Charles V of Spain, the nephew of Catherine, who was naturally a partisan of the unfortunate Queen.

In 1529, after considerable wrangling, the Pope consented to send a special envoy to England, with the power to summon a legatine court in an endeavour to establish and examine the true facts of the matter. The King so far suppressed his anger and royal dignity as to appear before the court, consisting of Cardinals Campeggio and Wolsey. But this availed him nothing, since the Pope, apparently concerned to delay judgement, somewhat suddenly transferred the case to Rome itself.

Henry, enraged at this obvious evidence of procrastination, deposed Wolsey from his high offices, and the disgraced Cardinal died soon afterwards. The King's next steps lay in the direction of the severance of the Church in England from the authority of the Pope. However, the King's measures were not hasty, but were rather designed to give the Pope pause for reflection. Henry's measured and deliberate actions reflect a man who was acting from motives of policy rather than conviction; he would apparently have avoided secession from Rome, had this course not proved necessary to obtain his divorce. Yet, in spite of persistent pressure, the Pope proved stubborn and unyielding.

In 1533, Thomas Cranmer, a man of Protestant sympathies, was appointed Archbishop of Canterbury. Later in the same year, Cranmer issued a decree of divorce to the King.

After Henry's marriage to Anne Boleyn, and her coronation as Queen, in June, 1533, the Pope excommunicated the King. The latter retaliated by passing an "Act of Supremacy", by which the last ties between the English Church and the See of Rome were severed without qualification.

Yet in spite of these shattering changes, it is noteworthy that Henry considered himself just as much a Catholic as he was before the separation from Rome. The only difference was that he had assumed the Pope's position as the head of the Church in England. Yet to some extent, however, the King could hardly fail to be influenced by the Reformation in continental Europe.

Question 3.

"More and his associates were uncompromising opponents of reform within the Church." Discuss briefly.

Answer

Sir Thomas More had received much of his early training in the humanistic circles of Oxford, was eventually called to the Bar, and ultimately entered the House of Commons. More's original claim to fame derived from his authority of "Utopia". The first part of this work consists of a searching criticism, of the political, social and religious ills of the England in which he lived; the second part suggests the remedies by describing life as lived in an imaginary, ideal Utopia.

John Colet, More's friend and colleague, was a scholar who distinguished himself at Oxford, both by his learning and his deep piety. In apparent protest against the theological complexities of contemporary

Church doctrine and dogma, he found himself attracted to St. Paul, whose directness and burning faith he greatly admired. An eloquent preacher, Colet eventually became Dean of St. Paul's Cathedral, in London. Here he founded a new boys' school, which he conducted personally on humanistic principles. Colet's address, in 1512, to the Convocation of the Church, roundly denounced both bishops and priests, resulting in a determined attempt to convict him of heresy.

In their attitude towards the Christian Church, the difference between Lollard and humanist was more than one degree. The aim of the Lollards was to destroy the Church as such, and obliterate its hierarchy. They desired, in fact, to establish their own sect. Such men as Colet and More, on the other hand, were concerned to introduce radical reforms within the framework of the existing Church. The subsequent career of More, who suffered martyrdom, rather than submit to the dictates of Henry VIII, amply supports this contention.

The English humanists had much in common with their fellows in Germany. They helped to pave the way towards religious and social reform before the Reformation actually took place. Moreover, they later protested against the Reformation not merely because of its violence and attendant bloodshed, but its theological aspects.

Question 4.

"There is evidence that, apart from the avowed hostility of the Lollards, the government and people of England, from the 14th century onwards, were resentful of many aspects of the Roman Catholic Church." Discuss.

Answer

While it is a truism to suggest that the Catholic Church derived its influence from the fact that it was an organization of those who professed the Christian faith, it is also true that its pre-eminent authority was related to the notion that it had been established by Christ himself, and was thus of divine origin. It is, moreover, a fundamental tenet of Christian faith that outside the Church there is no possibility of salvation - a proposition which, in earlier days, could not do otherwise than enhance the power and influence of Roman Catholicism.

Since, in pre-Renaissance times, the clergy were the most exalted, and (viewed broadly) the wealthiest class of society, it follows that they paid the price of power by undue exposure to temptation, and by adverse criticism, whether merited or not. Throughout the Middle Ages, prelates, abbots, priests and monks were subject to serious charges of bribery, corruption and immorality. While reforms were sometimes undertaken, the abuses recurred from time to time, whether in endemic or epidemic form, since even those who are nominally Christians are sometimes sinners, whether in large or small measure.

As early as the 14th century, the waxing national sentiment of the English people, coupled with a growing tendency to chafe against authority, found expression in actions directed against the Pope and the clergy. During the Hundred Years' War, opposition to Papal pronouncements, especially those relating to the taxation of the Church and clergy in England, reached a climax.

For some years the Pope had been resident at Avignon, in France. Since the Popes of the period were French, and a majority of the dignitaries of the Church likewise French, many Englishmen were persuaded that much of the Papal tax-money, ultimately derived from the public in England, was being used for the financial support of the French kingdom, with which the other was constantly at war, was not likely to commend itself to any part of the English nation.

It was in this spirit, that, in 1351, the Statute of Provisors was enacted, which prescribed that persons accepting Papal appointments to benefices in England were subject to imprisonment, and the forfeiture of their livings to the crown. In 1353, there followed the Statute of Praemunire, which decreed outlawry upon those who took legal suit in foreign courts.

In 1366, an even more significant expression of anti-Papal feeling was stated by the English Parliament. An annual tribute of a thousand marks, which had been promised by King John, was demanded by the Pope; it had not, in fact, been paid for some thirty years. In repudiating this demand, Parliament made it clear that no such payments might be made without the authority of both Houses of Parliament.

The Statute of Provisors was re-enacted in 1390 in more severe terms, while the Statute of Praemunire was re-enforced by further legislation in both 1365 and 1393.

Yet dissatisfaction with the dogma and the ritual of the Roman Church, and the worldly and sometimes scandalous lives of priests and prelates, was not confined to dissenting sects and ultra-patriotic groups. During the period of pacification which followed the conclusion of the Wars of the Roses, other elements came to be felt. English travellers and scholars, returning from the "Grand Tour" of the continent, tended to communicate some of the prevalent humanistic enthusiasm to their fellow countrymen. Eventually, the University of Oxford and, later, the University of Cambridge, became centres in which many humanistic ideas were eagerly discussed. In northern Europe, if one may generalise, the Renaissance was largely concerned with the sources of Christianity, rather than those of antiquity. Thus it was that Erasmus, the distinguished Netherlands scholar, was eagerly welcomed at Oxford in 1499, and on subsequent occasions before 1517. The importance of Erasmus to the English humanistic movement lies in the fact that he exerted a direct and profound influence on Sir Thomas More and John Colet—the two English men most concerned in what had come to be known as the "New Learning".

Question 5.

"The Duke of Norfolk wished to remain More's true and loyal friend." What evidence can be found in the play to support this assertion?

Answer

That the Duke of Norfolk wished to remain More's true and loyal friend would appear to be proven by the following points of evidence:

(a) Although More is not prepared to recommend Rich to him, but merely brings the young man to his notice, the Duke finds him employment. In so doing, he is evidently actuated by a desire to please More. (Act I, Scene 1).

(b) When the King is about to visit More at his Chelsea home, the Duke is much concerned by the fact that the other cannot be found until the last moment. Contending that More's casualness in his relationship with the King may militate to his disadvantage, he expresses himself forcibly both to Lady Alice and her husband. (Act I, Scene 6).

(c) The Duke is shown to be most disturbed when More resigns the Lord Chancellorship. (Act II, Scene 1).

(d) In conference with Cromwell at Hampton Court the Duke speaks repeatedly in More's defence. It is only when Cromwell speaks threateningly of the King's wishes, that he appears to give in to the matter of More's prosecution. (Act II, Scene 2).

(e) After the interrogation of More at Hampton Court, he deliberately seeks out his friend at the water-front and advises him to accede to the King's wishes. After More has deliberately insulted him, he shows considerable patience before finally losing his temper. (Act II, Scene 5).

(f)During the hearing of the Seventh Commission at the Tower, the Duke and Cromwell are on the verge of quarrelling openly. It appears that each is annoyed at the manner in which the other is questioning the accused man. (Act II, Scene 6).

(g) During More's trial for High Treason at Westminster, the Duke's manner towards More is much more considerate and restrained than that of Cromwell. He makes the point that More's life is in his own hands, as it has always been. (Act II, Scene 8).

(h) The Duke appears to be so nauseated by the proceedings that he forgets to offer More the chance of uttering a last word before sentence is pronounced. (Act II, Scene 8).

Question 6.

"Despite Cromwell's evident dislike for More and his principles, he is by no means anxious that the other's life should be sacrificed". What evidence may be found in support of this statement?

Answer

The following brief incidents are mentioned in support of the contention that Cromwell was not anxious that More's life should be sacrificed:

(a) At the public house known as "The Loyal Subject", Cromwell is at pains to obtain information from Rich which may be harmful to More. He believes, as he says, that Sir Thomas "could be frightened" into uttering support of the King's divorce. (Act I, Scene 7).

(b) In conversation with the Duke of Norfolk at Hampton Court, Cromwell makes it clear that he thinks that, "with a little pressure", More may be persuaded to support the King. Later, when talking to Rich, he states that if the "right law" cannot be found, one will have to be made. Here again, he appears to believe that More will prove sensible (Act II, Scene 2).

(c) Before interrogating More at Hampton Court, Cromwell makes it clear to him that he regrets his stubbornness adding that if he will change his mind, he will be handsomely rewarded by the King. Only after threatening More, without success, in the matter of the "Holy Maid of Kent", the King's "A Defence of the Seven Sacraments", and his attitude towards Henry's marriage to Anne Boleyn, does he begin to realize how inflexible More may prove. Later, in conversation with Rich, he admits that if Sir Thomas cannot be persuaded, then he must be destroyed. (Act II, Scene 4).

(d) At the conclusion of the hearing of the Seventh Commission, Cromwell's refusal to allow More to see his family, and his decision to take his books away from him, may be taken as evidence that he hopes thereby to break his will. (Act II, Scene 6).

(e) Norfolk and Cranmer having departed after the hearing of the Seventh Commission has been concluded, Cromwell is observed to be toying with a rack, and is evidently considering its use. He is then heard to mutter that the King would not permit it, and adds that a gentler way must be found. In either event, the object would have been the same - that of persuading More to recant. At this stage, it appears that Cromwell is somewhat uneasy as to his own future should he fail to force More into giving in. (Act II, Scene 6).

(f) During More's Trial for High Treason, Cromwell makes it abundantly clear that More's fate is in his own hands. He makes a point of mentioning that the charge against More is identical with that preferred against Fisher who was executed that very morning. Again, before the jury has considered its verdict, he tries to convey a message to More from the King himself, only to be halted abruptly by the accused man. (Act II, Scene 8).

Question 7.

What examples of "Alienation Effect" are to be found in the play?

Answer

The following are some examples of "Alienation Effect" to be found in the play:

(a) A large basket containing theatrical properties is shown on the stage (Act I, Scene 1)

(b) The Common Man, having spoken his introduction to the play proceeds to select a costume from the basket. Putting it on, he becomes More's Steward - a character within the play. (Act I, Scene 1) Thereafter, despite this fact, he speaks directly to the audience from time to time.

(c) There are no changes of scene in the conventional manner. The different sets are largely the result of controlled stage lighting, those parts of the stage that are not used as "acting areas" being blacked out as the occasion demands.

(d) Little or no attempt is made towards realism. The audience only becomes aware of the actors' supposed surroundings by the use of elementary symbols, as, for example, a painted screen suspended above the stage to indicate Hampton Court, flowered screens to represent the garden of More's Chelsea house, iron grills and a rack to denote the Tower of London, and a cage to represent More's cell.

(e) As the play proceeds, the Common Man assumes a variety of roles and guises. He is successively, More's steward, a boatman, an innkeeper, a jailer, the foreman of the jury, and the executioner.

(f) Perhaps the most obvious example of all occurs in Act II, Scene 8. The Common Man not only assumes the role of foreman of the jury, but the rest of the jurymen are not present, and are merely represented by folding stools, above which are suspended empty hats.

Question 8.

Explain the reference, in the opening Act of the play, to Machiavelli and his doctrines, and explain his significance.

Answer

Niccolo Machiavelli (1469—1527) was for several years secretary to the government of the Florentine Republic, at a period when the citizens of Florence were desperately striving to maintain the independence of their city-state..Machiavelli's observations of the political developments of his day were eventually embodied in a treatise named *The Prince*, published in 1516. Machiavelli contended that the day of small political units had passed, and that the future of Europe belonged to the absolute monarch. He was fired by the success of such men as Louis XII of France, Ferdinand of Aragon and Caesar Borgia, contending that only under such rulers might the state become unified, and contentious social classes made subject to a common and all-embracing law. Machiavelli was fully aware of the methods that such rulers pursued to achieve their ends, no matter how deceitful, violent and unscrupulous. However, Machiavelli did not invent, but merely described the methods of crafty deception that were successful in the Europe in which he lived. In recent days. *The Prince* has come to be known as "A Handbook for Dictators", and it is believed to have inspired both Hitler and Mussolini.

Rich's cynical remark, at the outset of the play, to the effect that "every man has his price", although commonly credited to Walpole (1676—1745), is typically Machiavellian in spirit. Meaning that a man may be induced to do anything, provided that he be offered a sufficient reward, Rich's words express aptly his own personal philosophy. More, of course, disagrees with Rich. The attitudes of the two men are amply borne out by the subsequent events of the play. Rich, for his part, demonstrates that he cannot withstand temptation, even at the expense of a friend and benefactor. On the other hand, More's own fate is adequate proof that some men cannot be bought even when offered substantial inducements at the hands of a King.

Apart from Rich, three other characters in the play — Wolsey, Cromwell and Chapuys - display Machiavellian cynicism and craft. Wolsey and Cromwell are entirely frank in their contention that what the King wants, he must be enabled to obtain. Chapuys, for his part, is anxious to further the interests of his royal master, Charles V of Spain, and the Roman Catholic Church. In doing so, he does not scruple to solicit More's support, being apparently unaware of the Englishman's sturdy patriotism.

It is significant that, while belonging to opposite camps, Cromwell and Chapuys are observed to leave the scene of execution together, with arms linked. They evidently have something in common - the simple conviction that martyrdom is unnecessary and should be avoided.

Question 9.

(a) Explain what is meant by the classical conception of a tragic hero.

(b) State whether or not Sir Thomas More may be regarded as a tragic hero, and give reasons in support of your conclusion.

Answer

(a) The classical conception of a tragic hero, as expounded by Aristotle, may be explained as follows:

(i) The Tragic hero must be a man of illustrious or superior rank.

(ii) He must not be a perfectly good man, since his downfall would merely shock us by its improbability.

(iii) He must not be an utterly bad man, since not only would his downfall fail to inspire pity and terror, but would appear appropriate and well-merited.

(iv) He must be a man "not absolutely or eminently good or wise, who is brought to disaster, not by sheer depravity, but by some error or frailty".

(b) In terms of the above conception, Sir Thomas More may reasonably be regarded as a tragic hero because:

(i) More was obviously a man of illustrious rank—the former Lord Chancellor of the realm.

(ii) Although a very good man, More was not a "perfectly" good man. He had led a somewhat dissolute youth, and showed an almost violent bias towards "heretics". Yet he was held in such general high esteem that, in fact, his downfall does shock us by its improbability.

(iii) He was obviously not a bad man, while his downfall appears inappropriate and ill-merited, and cannot fail to inspire pity and terror.

(iv) More was "not absolutely or eminently good or wise", and the cause of his disaster was demonstrably not depravity. However, that his singlemindedness may be construed as error or frailty, is a dubious suggestion.

Question 10.

What is the irony of More's association with Rich?

Answer

The irony of More's association with Rich is demonstrated by the following facts:

(a) At the outset of the play, More shows himself to be kind and helpful towards the ambitious young man. He presents him with a beautiful and valuable Italian cup, advises him strongly to take a teaching post that he has found for him, and finally brings him to the notice of the Duke of Norfolk, with the object of finding him employment, (Act I, Scene 1).

(b) Later, at "The Loyal Subject", Rich is persuaded to reveal to Cromwell the circumstances in which More had given him the Italian cup, and how the matter might be authenticated. (Act I, Scene 7). That Cromwell has taken pains to use the matter of the cup as a means of bringing pressure on More is shown during his discussion with Norfolk at Hampton Court, when Catherine Anger offers her evidence. Afterwards, during the same scene, it appears entirely evident that Rich will not scruple to help Cromwell to the fullest extent in his prosecution of More. (Act II, Scene 2) Rich's final act of ingratitude and infamy towards his former friend and patron occurs in the Trial Scene. In support of Cromwell's case against More, Rich gives perjured evidence to the effect that the accused man had denied the competance of Parliament to pass the Act of Supremacy. (Act II, Scene 8)

Question 11.

"It is difficult to understand why More accepted the office of Lord Chancellor of England, when it appeared obvious that Parliament was being called together to put into effect the very measures of which he disapproved." Discuss.

Answer

More accepted the office of Lord Chancellor on 26 October, 1529, in succession to Cardinal Wolsey, who regarded him as his most eligible successor.

Sir Thomas was certainly aware of the likely trend of events, and would perhaps have declined the appointment, had he been able to do so. However, it appears certain that he had no choice in the matter, since, as an official of the King's service, he was no longer a free agent.

He had previously made it clear to the King that he could not change his attitude in the matter of the divorce. It is commonly believed that the King promised to permit him freedom of conscience, and to employ him in no matters which touched on the highly controversial question of his divorce. If this were so, then clearly More had no alternative but to obey the request of his royal master.

All the time that More was Lord Chancellor, the King refrained from employing him on any business relating to his divorce and re-marriage, since he was well aware that Sir Thomas disapproved of his intentions. There is evidence, however, that after accepting his high office, More was again approached by the King, in an effort to persuade him to change his mind, but without avail.

It may be wondered why a man of Henry's character did not simply demand of More his acceptance in the matter of the divorce. The explanation appears to be that his promise of liberty of conscience to his servants was one of the most powerful weapons that he could wield. It enabled him to insist on their serving him so long as he needed and desired their services. He might later play upon their gratitude to exact compliance with his wishes - compliance which he might never have been able to exact by force. But if this device failed, the King might finally resort to a strong threat, such as was made to More (Act II, Scene 4) when Cromwell told him: "Then know that the King commands me to charge you in his name with great ingratitude! And to tell you that there never was nor never could be so villainous a servant nor so traitorous a subject as yourself!"

Question 12.

At the conclusion of More's interrogation by the Seventh Commission, Cromwell refuses permission for his family to visit him, and gives orders that his books must be removed. (Act II, Scene 6) Yet it is evident from subsequent scenes that his family is allowed to visit him, although his books are, in fact, removed. Explain the apparent inconsistency of these facts.

Answer

The apparent inconsistencies suggested in the above question may be explained as follows:

(a) At the conclusion of Act II, Scene 6, Cromwell is observed to be toying with a rack, as though he is considering its use to force Sir Thomas to do the King's will. He is then heard to mutter that a gentler way must be found.

(b) One aspect of Cromwell's "gentler way" is revealed in Act II, Scene 7. During More's brief re-union with his family, it becomes clear that the real object of the visit is that Lady Margaret (who has taken an oath to this effect) should persuade her father to change his mind and accede to the King's wishes.

(c) The reason that More's books are, in fact, taken away from him, is to give Rich the opportunity to interrogate More, and trick him into a treasonable admission. In the event, More is not tricked by Rich, whereupon the latter overcomes the difficulty by recourse to perjury. These facts are made clear during More's trial for High Treason. (Act II, Scene 8)

Textual Quotations

Identify each of the following quotations by reference to the speaker, the person addressed (where applicable) and the place where the conversation takes place. Include in your answer brief details describing the circumstances in which the speech is made.

Question 13.

"The oath was put to good and faithful subjects up and down the country and they had declared His Grace's Title to be just and good. And when it came to the prisoner he refused. He calls this silence". (Act II, Scene 8)

Answer

Cromwell is addressing the court at More's trial for High Treason at Westminster. More having declined to swear an oath to the effect that he supports the King's title to be Supreme Head of the Church in England, Cromwell is arguing that his silence in the matter is tantamount to opposition.

Question 14.

"Some men think the earth is round, others think it flat; it is a matter capable of question. But if it is flat, will the King's command make it round? And if it is round, will the King's command flatten it?" (Act II, Scene 6)

Answer

More is replying to Cranmer during his appearance before the Seventh Commission at the Tower of London, Cranmer having told the other that he undoubtedly owes obedience to the King, and that he should therefore give his oath in support of the Act of Succession. More agrees with the first point, but disagrees with the second. His failure to comply derives from his conviction that scruples of conscience cannot be altered by roval order.

Question 15.

"We couldn't come so deep into your confidence as to know these reasons why a man in poverty can't take four thousand pounds." (Act II, Scene 3)

Answer

Lady Alice is addressing her husband at their house in Chelsea. More had previously resigned the Lord Chancellorship, and the family is in financial difficulties. Aware of this fact, the Clergy in Convocation offered More a gift of four thousand pounds, which he declined on the grounds that his acceptance of it might be misconstrued.

Question 16.

"Oh, alas, as I think of it I see so clearly that I can not come with Your Grace, that my endeavour is not to think at all". (Act I, Scene 6)

Answer

More is speaking to King Henry, on the occasion of the latter's visit to his house at Chelsea. The King has just asked him if he has given any recent thought to the matter of his divorce. More's distressful reply appears to mean that he is so deeply conscious of his attitude, that he would prefer not to think of it.

Question 17.

"For seven months, that's two hundred days, I have to show: the acquaintance of the Cardinal's outer doorman, the indifference of the Cardinal's inner doorman, and the Cardinal's chamberlain's hand in my chest!" (Act I, Scene 1)

Answer

At More's house at Chelsea, Rich is complaining bitterly to More of his lack of success in obtaining an audience of Cardinal Wolsey. His remark serves to demonstrate his determination to bring himself to the notice of the great. Moreover, it indicates the pomp and ceremony with which Wolsey surrounded himself at Hampton Court.

Question 18.

"If you could just see facts flat on, without that moral squint; with just a little common sense, you could have been a statesman." (Act I, Scene 2)

Answer

At Hampton Court Palace, Cardinal Wolsey is addressing More. He has just asked the other what he thinks of a despatch that he proposes to send to the Pope, asking that King Henry's marriage to Catherine of Aragon be declared invalid. More, having vouchsafed a non-committal reply, followed by the suggestion that the King's Council should be informed of the contents of the document, the Cardinal responds in the words quoted.

Question 19.

"May I say I am sure my master's admiration will not be diminished." (Act I, Scene 3)

Answer

Chapuys makes this remark to More, when paying him what he terms "an unofficial visit" at his house at Chelsea. He has attempted to deliver More a letter from his master, King Charles V of Spain. More, however, refuses to accept the letter, and asks his wife and daughter to testify to the fact that it remains unopened, and that the seals are intact.

Question 20.

"Doesn't know how to be frightened? Why, then he never put his hand in a candle....did he? (Act I, Scene 7)

Answer

Cromwell makes this remark to Rich after they have been speaking together at an inn, *The Loyal Subject*. After prevailing upon Rich to disclose the circumstances in which More made him the gift of an Italian silver cup, the young man asserts that More is "an innocent", who is incapable of being frightened. Seizing Rich, Cromwell holds his hand in a candle flame for a moment, at the same time uttering the remark quoted.

Question 21.

"In the May of 1526 the King published a book, a theological work. It was called *A Defence of the Seven Sacraments.*" (Act II, Scene 4)

Answer

This remark was made by Cromwell to More during his initial interrogation at Hampton Court. More having maintained a stony and non-committal silence in response to Cromwell's accusations the latter then tells him that the King is not pleased with him. Cromwell proceeds to make certain accusations against More, one of which is to the effect that *A Defence of Seven Sacraments* was, in fact, written by More. The accused man denies this, stating that he merely answered certain questions concerning canon law that the King put to him.

Question 22.

"And if anyone wants my opinion of the King and his Council they've only to ask for it." (Act II, Scene 7)

Answer

Lady Alice makes this remark to her husband when she is visiting him during his imprisonment at the Tower of London. She has previously told More that, although she cannot understand or sympathize with his stubbornness, he is nevertheless the best man that she has ever met or is likely to meet. In a spirited outburst, she then makes the remark quoted.

Question 23.

"You must relieve yourself of our friendship. No one's safe now, and you have a son." (Act II, Scene 5)

Answer

These words are spoken by More to the Duke of Norfolk, after the latter has sought him out by the Thames-side, subsequent to his initial interrogation by Cromwell at Hampton Court. Norfolk has pleaded with him to change his mind for the sake of his friends. More however, is firm, and then utters the remark quoted. The Duke having reiterated his friendship, More deliberately insults him. While prepared to suffer himself, he clearly does not wish his friends to be victimised by reason of their association with him.

Question 24.

"But what matters to me is not whether it's true or not but that I believe it to be true, or rather not that I *believe* it, but that *I* believe it....I trust I make myself obscure." (Act II, Scene 1)

Answer

More utters this remark to the Duke of Norfolk, during a long conversation at his home at Chelsea. Norfolk has just brought the news of the "Submission of the Clergy", whereupon More has divested himself of his chain of office as Lord Chancellor. This utterance is especially noteworthy, since it reveals what the author terms More's "adamantine sense of his own self."

Suggested Additional Questions

Question 25.

"More displays a keen sense of humour, even in adverse circumstances." Discuss this contention, giving specific instances in support of your answer.

Question 26.

What examples of symbolism are to be found in the play? Explain the significance of each.

Question 27.

Contrast and compare the character and personality of More with that of his son-in-law, Roper.

Question 28.

"Undoubtedly, Rich is the arch-villain of the play". State if you agree with this assertion, giving reasons for your answer.

Question 29.

"Although Cromwell has little alternative but to press charges against More, he appears uneasy of the outcome." Why, in your opinion is this so?

Question 30.

At least one of the scenes in the play is contrived so as to afford some measure of comic relief. Identify such a scene, and write a summary of it.

Question 31.

Quote from the play in support of the contention that Lady Alice, while deeply fond of her husband, is nevertheless exasperated by him.

Question 32.

Describe the quarrel between More and Norfolk. State which man you think the more blameworthy, giving reasons to support your answer.

Question 33.

Describe how Lady Margaret strives to induce her father to change his mind. How, in spite of her manifest desire to help him, does she add to his distress of spirit?

Question 34.

What is your view of the fact that the Common Man takes several parts within the play? Would it not have been better, in your estimation, if the playwright had followed a more conventional plan?

Question 35.

More evidently believes himself to be a man of caution. State if you agree with his view of himself, giving reasons in support of your answer.

Question 36.

What reasons had King Henry for desiring a divorce? Which, in your estimation, were the most valid, and which the least? Justify your contentions.

NOTES